Your Rights
2002-03

A GUIDE TO MONEY BENEFITS FOR OLDER PEOPLE

Sally West

BOOKS

Age Concern would like to thank the Department for Work and Pensions and the Department of Health for their comments on the text. The author also thanks colleagues in Age Concern England's Communications Division for their contributions.

Published by Age Concern England
1268 London Road
London SW16 4ER

© 2002 Age Concern England

Thirtieth Edition

This edition prepared by Sally West

Editor Ro Lyon
Production Vinnette Marshall
Typeset by GreenGate Publishing Services, Tonbridge, Kent
Printed in Great Britain by Bell & Bain Ltd, Glasgow

A catalogue record for this book is available from the British Library

ISBN 0-86242-360-0 hardback
ISBN 0-86242-351-1 paperback

Bulk orders
Age Concern England is pleased to offer customised editions of all its titles to UK companies, institutions or other organisations wishing to make a bulk purchase. For further information, please contact the Publishing Department at the address on this page. Tel: 020 8765 7200. Fax: 020 8765 7211. Email: books@ace.org.uk

CONTENTS

INTRODUCTION

This book provides information about the main financial benefits available for older people. Most of the social security rates given apply from the week beginning 8 April 2002.

Your Rights is divided into five parts. The first section gives details about pensions and retirement, and the second section is about financial help for those on low incomes. The third section covers benefits for disabled people and their carers, while the fourth gives information about other types of financial help, including the system of help towards paying for care.

Many of the subjects covered in *Your Rights* can be complicated, and the book aims to explain them as simply as possible. However, it cannot cover all situations and circumstances. If you need more information, the fifth section gives details about obtaining relevant leaflets from the Department for Work and Pensions (formerly called the Department of Social Security), Age Concern factsheets and contacting other local and national sources of help. There is also an index and a summary of main benefit rates on page 168.

Please note that although some older people have young families, benefits for children are not covered in this book.

During 2001 the Department for Work and Pensions (DWP) replaced the Department for Social Security (DSS) as the government department responsible for State pensions and benefits. It is likely, however, that people will still refer to the DSS for some time and that it will still be mentioned in old leaflets or other written materials. Another major change is that from April 2001 the Benefits Agency and Employment Service have been replaced by the Pensions Service and Jobcentre Plus. There is more information about this on page 144. Throughout this book when we refer to the 'social security office' this will generally be the local Jobcentre Plus office for people of working age. For older people it will be the local Pension Service, which, as explained on page 144, may be based in places accessible to older people rather than always in social security offices.

Where you live

All the information covered in *Your Rights* applies to people living in England. It also applies to Scotland and Wales except where differences are pointed out in the text.

Although there is a separate social security system in Northern Ireland, the social security benefits available are generally the same. However, there may be some differences in the sources of financial help discussed in the section 'Other Financial Benefits' and local and national sources of further information will also be different.

For further information or advice relating to older people living in Scotland, Wales and Northern Ireland, contact Age Concern Scotland, Cymru or Northern Ireland – the addresses are on page 157. Age Concern Scotland produces its own edition of *Your Rights*.

For more information on pensions and benefits for people living abroad, either permanently or temporarily, contact your local social security office (if you are currently in this country) or the Pensions and Overseas Benefits Directorate, Tyneview Park, Whitley Road, Benton, Newcastle Upon Tyne NE98 1BA; this is the part of the Department for Work and Pensions (DWP) that deals with pensions and benefits paid abroad. It produces a series of leaflets covering social security arrangements with countries outside the UK including Jersey, Guernsey and the countries of the European Union.

If you are living in the UK but subject to immigration control your benefit postion may be affected. This book does not provide information about immigration status, so contact a local advice agency if you need further details.

Keeping up to date and the April 2002 Budget

This book is based on information available at the beginning of March 2002 and should apply until the beginning of April 2003. However, sometimes changes are announced during the year and this year the Budget is later than usual (17 April 2002). State pension and benefit rates are announced in the Autumn, so it is not expected that the Budget will make major changes to the information in this book. To check whether there are any changes, you can ring Freephone 0800 00 99 66 and ask for the free *Your Rights Budget Update*, or you can fill in the form on page 156.

A number of proposed changes are mentioned in *Your Rights*. If you need information about the latest position or you have questions on any specific points in the book, please write to Age Concern England at the address on page 157.

A new edition of *Your Rights* will be available in April 2003 – please let us know if you have any comments or suggestions.

Pensions, Bereavement Benefits and Retirement

This part of Your Rights *contains information about the State Retirement Pension. There is also a section which describes the benefits available to people who are not in work before State Pension age, and another which looks at the effect on State benefits if you choose to work after pension age. In addition there are details about bereavement benefits; the Christmas Bonus (paid to people receiving a State Pension or certain other benefits); the procedure for appealing against a social security decision; and occupational and personal pensions.*

The State Retirement Pension is paid to people who have reached State Pension age (60 for women, 65 for men) and who fulfil the National Insurance (NI) contribution conditions. The amount you receive is not affected by your income and savings but it is taxable.

Your pension may consist of a Basic Pension plus an Additional Pension (based on contributions after April 1978) and a Graduated Pension (based on contributions between April 1961 and April 1975). You will receive an extra 25p when you reach the age of 80. You may also receive extra pension if you defer drawing your pension. These different parts of the pension are explained below.

Whether you are entitled to a State Pension or not, you may be able to claim other benefits such as Income Support (Minimum Income Guarantee), Housing Benefit and Council Tax Benefit, which depend on your income and savings.

See social security guide NP 46 about Retirement Pensions.

Equalisation of State Pension age

Parliament has passed legislation to equalise State Pension age at 65 for both men and women. This is to be phased in over ten years starting in 2010. No one born before 6 April 1950 will be affected by these changes.

BASIC PENSION

The Basic Pension is paid at the same rate to everyone who has fulfilled the NI contribution conditions. The full weekly rates are shown below:

Single person	£75.50
Wife on husband's contributions	£45.20
Married couple on husband's contributions	£120.70
Married couple (if both paid full contributions)	£151.00

Who qualifies?

You will receive the full basic rate of pension if you have paid, or been credited with, NI contributions at the full rate for most of the years of your working life. If you have not paid enough, you may get a reduced pension or you may not get a pension at all (see 'Your contributions', pages 7–9).

Normally you need to have satisfied the contribution conditions in your own right; but married women, divorcees or widowed people may be able to claim a pension on their spouse's or ex-spouse's contributions, as explained in the following pages.

Pensions for married women

If you are a married woman and you have paid full contributions for all of your working life, you should be entitled to the Basic Pension of £75.50 a week when you become 60. If you have paid full contributions for only part of your working life, you may be entitled to a reduced pension. However, any years when you were paying the married woman's reduced-rate contributions will not count towards a pension.

If you are 60 or over but have not paid enough contributions for a pension in your own right, you cannot get any Basic Pension until your husband draws his. When your husband draws his pension, you should claim the married woman's pension, which will be £45.20 a week if your husband has a full contribution record.

If at the age of 60 you are entitled to a pension on your own contributions of less than £45.20 a week, it will be made up to a maximum of £45.20 a week when your husband draws his pension. You will need to make a claim. However, if your own pension is more than £45.20 a week, you cannot get any extra pension based on your husband's contributions.

On top of any basic pension you receive, you may also be entitled to Graduated and/or Additional Pension based on any contributions you have made, as explained on pages 15 and 20.

Sometimes **married women** who have paid NI contributions in the past but who are not working when they reach 60, do not realise that they may be entitled to some pension based on their earlier contributions. The pension is not awarded automatically – you have to make a claim. So if you think you may be entitled to a pension, and you have not been sent a claim pack, contact your local social security office. However you should be aware that if you are already receiving a pension or another benefit, for example a pension based on your husband's contributions or a Widow's Pension, you may not be entitled to anything more.

Increases for dependants

Dependent wives

If you are under 60 when your husband draws his pension (at 65 or more), he may be able to claim for you as a dependant, and his pension will be increased by a maximum of £45.20 a week. However, your husband will not receive any increase for you if you receive certain State benefits of £45.20 or more. The increase may also be affected by any earnings you have.

If you live with your husband, he will not be able to receive the increase if you are working and earn more than £53.95 a week (after certain expenses connected with work have been deducted). Any occupational or personal pension you receive will be counted as earnings. If you do not live with your husband, he will not be able to receive this increase if you earn more than £45.20 a week.

Dependent husbands

If you are a married man and your wife is receiving a State Pension, she may be able to get an increase for you of up to £45.20, provided you are not earning more than £53.95 a week (£45.20 if you do not live with your wife). However, she can get this increase only if she is receiving Incapacity Benefit with an addition for you immediately before she starts to draw the

State Pension. Your wife will not receive any increase if you have a State Pension or certain other benefits of £45.20 or more.

Pensions for divorced and separated people

Divorced people

If you are divorced but do not qualify for a full pension based on your own contributions, you may be able to use your former spouse's contribution record to increase the amount of Basic Pension you receive to a maximum of the single person's pension of £75.50 a week. You are not entitled to your former spouse's Graduated or Additional Pension. (However, since December 2000, when rules on 'pension sharing' came into effect, it has been possible for Additional Pension to be divided as part of a divorce settlement.)

You can substitute your former spouse's contribution record for your own from the start of your working life up until your divorce or just for the period of your marriage.

If you get divorced before pension age, you may need to pay further contributions after your divorce to qualify for a Basic Pension. If you get divorced after pension age and are receiving the married woman's pension, you may be able to use the rules outlined above to get a full pension.

If you remarry before pension age, you cannot claim a pension on your former husband's or wife's contributions. However, if you remarry after pension age you will not lose a pension based on your previous spouse's contributions.

See Inland Revenue leaflet CA 10 which gives information for divorced women.

Separated women

If you are separated and do not qualify for a Basic Pension on your own contributions when you reach 60 or you are only entitled to a pension of less than £45.20, you may be able to claim the married woman's pension of up to £45.20 a week when your husband claims his.

Retirement Pensions for widows and widowers

This section looks at the amount of Retirement Pension that a widow or widower can receive at State Pension age. For information about benefits for widows and widowers who are under pension age, see pages 28–30.

Widows

If you were under 60 when your husband died and you have not remarried, you may be entitled to the State Pension based on his contributions and/or your own, once you reach pension age. The amount you receive will depend upon your own, and your late husband's, contribution record and the age at which you were widowed. If you were 60 or over when your husband died, and not receiving the full Basic Pension, you may be able to use his contribution record to bring your Basic Pension up to a maximum of £75.50.

You may also receive Additional Pension and/or Graduated Pension based on your husband's contributions, as explained on pages 18–19 and 20.

Once you are drawing the State Pension at age 60 or over, you can remarry or live with a man as his wife without losing a pension based on your previous husband's contributions.

Widowers

If you were widowed on or after 6 April 1979 and do not have enough contributions of your own, you may be entitled to a Retirement Pension based on your wife's contributions provided you were both over pension age when she died.

You may also inherit some of your wife's Additional Pension and/or Graduated Pension as explained on pages 19 and 20. If you do not fulfil the above conditions, perhaps because you were widowed before age 65, once you reach pension age you may be able to substitute your wife's contribution record for your own in order to increase your Basic Pension up to a maximum of £75.50 a week. Once you are receiving the pension at age 65 or over you will not lose any pension based on your former wife's contributions if you remarry.

Your contributions

This section explains the contribution conditions for the Basic Pension. Your contribution record will depend on the NI contributions you have paid and any 'credits' you received for periods when you could not work.

Until April 2000 people paid NI contributions if their earnings were equal to or above a certain level known as the 'Lower Earnings Limit'. Since April 2000 the starting point for paying contributions has been higher than the Lower Earnings Limit. This year, 2002–2003, the Lower Earnings Limit is £75 a week but the threshold for paying NI contributions is £89. However, if you have earnings between £75 and £89 you will be treated as though you are paying NI contributions and will still be building up entitlement to the Basic Pension and other contributory benefits. When reference is made in this book to people who have 'paid' NI contributions, this includes people with earnings between £75 and £89 a week.

There are two conditions that you must meet in order to receive a pension. The first condition is that you have paid sufficient contributions during at least one year in your working life since 6 April 1975 or paid at least 50 flat-rate contributions at any time before 6 April 1975. Credited contributions cannot count towards this first condition.

The second condition is that to receive a full Basic Pension you must have paid or been credited with contributions for most of the years of your working life. To receive any Basic Pension at all you must have a minimum number of years' contributions.

Whether you will get a full pension depends on your 'working life' and 'qualifying years', and whether your contribution record has been protected by 'credits' and/or 'Home Responsibilities Protection'. These terms are explained below.

If you are more than four months away from pension age, you can check whether you have paid enough contributions to get a full pension by completing form BR 19, obtainable from your local social security office.

Both men and women aged 80 or over who have not paid enough contributions for a Basic Pension might qualify for the non-contributory pension described on page 20.

How are contributions paid?

Since April 1975 employed people have paid contributions as a percentage of earnings, and these are collected with Income Tax. Self-employed people pay flat-rate contributions each week which count towards the Basic Pension. If your taxable income is over a certain amount, extra contributions will be collected with your Income Tax.

Which contributions count?

If you paid the married woman's or widow's reduced-rate contributions, these do not count towards a pension in your own right. Contributions made abroad may help you qualify for the Basic Pension provided the country where you worked has a reciprocal agreement with the UK.

See Inland Revenue leaflet NI 38 for information about social security abroad.

Working life

Your 'working life' is the period on which your contribution record is based. This normally starts in the tax year (ie 6 April to 5 April) when you were 16 and ends with the last full tax year before your 60th (women) or 65th (men) birthday. A woman reaching pension age now has a working life of 44 years and a man reaching pension age now has a working life of 49 years.

However, if you were over 16 when the National Insurance scheme started in 1948, you may have a shorter working life – see social security guide NP 46.

Qualifying years

A 'qualifying year' is a tax year in which you have paid (or been credited with) enough contributions to go towards a pension.

Since 1978 a 'qualifying year' has been one in which contributions are paid on earnings which are the same as, or more than, 52 times the weekly Lower Earnings Limit. (Between April 1975 and April 1978 the qualifying earnings were 50 times the Lower Earnings Limit.) This tax year, 2002–2003, the Lower Earnings Limit is £75 a week.

Before 1975 working people paid contributions by weekly stamp. To work out your qualifying years before 1975, all your stamps (paid and credited) are added up and divided by 50, rounding up any that are left over – but you cannot have more qualifying years worked out in this way than the number of years in your working life up to April 1975.

See Inland Revenue leaflets CA 01 (NI for employees) and CA 02 (NI for self-employed people).

Credits

If you are under pension age (60 for women, 65 for men), you may receive a credit in place of an NI contribution for each week you register for Jobseeker's Allowance and are seeking work or you are unable to work because you are sick or disabled or you are receiving Invalid Care Allowance. Men aged 60–64 who are not paying contributions will normally receive credits automatically even if they are not ill or signing on as unemployed. However, men cannot get these automatic credits for any tax year during which they are abroad for more than six months.

Late and voluntary contributions

If there are periods when you will not be paying contributions, perhaps because you will be abroad, you may want to consider paying voluntary contributions to protect your pension record. If there are gaps in your contribution record, it is sometimes possible to pay late contributions. However, these must normally be paid by the end of the sixth tax year after the one in which they are due. Ask at your social security office if you need advice.

See Inland Revenue leaflets CA 08 (on voluntary contributions) and CA 07 (on late contributions).

Calculating your pension

To be entitled to a full Basic Pension, about nine out of every ten years of your working life have to be qualifying years. This means that women with a working life of 44 years will need 39 qualifying years for a full pension. Men with a working life of 49 years will need 44 qualifying years for a full pension.

If you are not entitled to the full Basic Pension, you may get a reduced one provided you have at least a quarter of the qualifying years you need for a full pension.

Example

Christina Paretsky was born on 10 August 1942 and was 16 in 1958. Her working life runs from 6 April 1958 to 5 April 2002, a total of 44 years. To receive a full Basic Pension, she needs 39 or more qualifying years. If she has worked and paid contributions for only 20 years of her working life, she will receive about half the Basic Pension.

Home Responsibilities Protection

Home Responsibilities Protection (HRP) started in 1978 to protect the contribution record of people caring for a child or a sick or disabled person.

You cannot get HRP for the years when you were looking after someone before April 1978. A married woman or widow cannot get HRP for any tax year in which she, if she was working, would only be due to pay reduced-rate NI contributions.

You are entitled to HRP if you meet any of the following conditions, or a combination of them, for a whole tax year (but note that the rules changed in 1988 for the third condition):

- You get Child Benefit for a child under 16.
- You get Income Support because you are looking after someone and therefore do not need to register for Jobseeker's Allowance.
- For at least 35 hours a week you look after someone who receives, for a minimum of 48 weeks in the year, Attendance Allowance, the middle or highest rate of the care component of Disability Living Allowance, or Constant Attendance Allowance. For tax years before 6 April 1988, the allowance had to be paid for 52 weeks.

If you get Invalid Care Allowance, you will normally be getting credits towards your pension so you will not need HRP, although you cannot get credits if you retained the right to pay the married woman's reduced-rate contributions.

How to work it out

HRP makes it easier for you to qualify for a Basic Pension. Each year of 'home responsibility' will be taken away from the number of qualifying years you need to get a full pension. However, HRP cannot be used to reduce the number of qualifying years to below 20.

Example

Eileen Smith, who was born in 1942, started work at 16 and paid full contributions for 30 years until 1988 when she gave up work to look after her mother. She was still caring for her mother when she became 60 in 2002 so her pension was worked out in the following way:

Working life	44 years
Number of qualifying years needed for a full pension	39 years
Number of years of HRP	14 years
Number of qualifying years needed for a full pension after taking away years of HRP	25 years

Normally Eileen would need to have paid contributions for 39 years in order to receive a full pension. However, because her 14 years of HRP reduce the number of qualifying years she needs to 25, she is entitled to the full Basic Pension although she has paid only 30 years of contributions.

When to claim

HRP should be given automatically if you qualify under the first two conditions described above. You should not have to claim.

You must claim HRP if you qualify under the third condition – because you are looking after someone who is getting one of the allowances mentioned above, such as Attendance Allowance – or if you qualify under one condition for part of the tax year and under another for the rest of the year. For years from April 2002 onwards you will need to claim by the end of the third year following the year for which you are claiming HRP. Ask for claim form CF 411 from your social security office.

How to claim your pension

About four months before you reach pension age you should be sent a claim pack. You can ring 0845 300 1084 to make a claim over the phone or to ask for a claim form. If you have not been contacted about claiming your pension three months before your birthday, contact the local social security office or ring 0845 300 1084. A married woman claiming a pension on her husband's contributions will need to make a separate claim.

You may decide not to draw your pension at 60 (women) or 65 (men) in order to gain extra pension, in which case, when you wish to start claiming the pension, you should contact your local office well in advance. Deferring your pension is explained on pages 21–23.

Once you reach the age of 65 (women) or 70 (men), you should claim your pension as you will gain no further increases.

If you make a late claim for your pension, it can only be backdated for up to three months.

How your pension is paid

There are two ways to have your pension paid. You may choose to collect it each week at a post office, in which case your pension is paid one week in advance. If you cannot get to a post office, someone else can cash your pension for you. The pension book explains how this is done.

If you prefer to have your pension paid into a bank, building society account, or post office account, you can have it paid directly by 'automated credit transfer'; the money will then normally be paid in arrears and you can choose to receive it either four-weekly or quarterly. However, if you receive Income Support (Minimum Income Guarantee) this can be paid together with your pension by automated credit transfer, weekly in advance.

The Government wants to move towards a system where payments are generally made into bank and building society accounts. It has said, however, that people will still be able to collect their pension or benefit in cash at the post office if they choose to do so and that arrangements will be made for people without bank accounts. The change is due to be phased in between 2003 and 2005. For more information contact Age Concern England at the address on page 157.

Pay-day for anyone who started to draw their pension before 28 September 1984 is normally Thursday. For people who retired after that date, pay-day is usually Monday, although if your spouse is already receiving a pension on Thursday, you can choose to have yours on the same day. You cannot receive any pension for days of retirement before your first pay-day.

Most pensions of £5 a week or less are paid once a year, in
December, in arrears. If you requested payment by automated
credit transfer, you will be paid by that method; if you requested
payment by order book, you will be paid by crossed payable order.

See social security leaflet BR 436A (payments into accounts).

Going abroad or living there

If you receive your pension by weekly order book and are going
abroad for less than three months, you can cash your pension
orders when you come home. However, a pension order cannot
be cashed more than three months after the date printed on it.
If you are going abroad for longer, tell your local social security
office well in advance so that your pension can be paid into a
bank or other account while you are away. Alternatively, you
may arrange for your pension to accrue and be paid in one
lump sum on your return. If you do not receive your pension
by weekly order book, you do not need to tell your local office
unless you are staying abroad for more than six months. You
can, if you wish, arrange to receive your pension in the country
where you are staying. If you remain abroad, the annual
pension increase will be paid only if you are living in a
European Union country or in a country with which the UK has
special arrangements.

Contact your local social security office or the Pensions and
Overseas Benefits Directorate, Tyneview Park, Whitley Road,
Benton, Newcastle Upon Tyne NE98 1BA.

Going into hospital

If you go into hospital, you will receive your full pension for up
to six weeks. (The Government has announced that this will be
increased to 13 weeks, probably in October 2003.) After that, if
you are single, your pension is usually reduced by a set amount
which, at the time of writing, was expected to be £28.70. If you
are still in hospital after one year it will be reduced to only
£15.10 a week.

If you are married and your husband or wife is at home, he or she will be considered as your 'dependant'. When you have a dependant, your pension is reduced by £15.10 a week after six weeks in hospital. After a year, your pension will be reduced by a further £15.10 a week. You will normally be paid £15.10 of the pension and, if you agree, any remaining pension will be paid to your dependant.

See social security leaflet GL 12.

If you disagree with a decision

If you think that you have been awarded the wrong amount of pension, or disagree with another decision to do with your pension, you can either ask for the decision to be revised or appeal against it. Further details are given on pages 32–35.

ADDITIONAL PENSION

If you have worked and paid contributions since 6 April 1978, when you receive your Retirement Pension it may include some Additional Pension on top of any Basic Pension you receive. This is taxable and based on earnings. You may qualify for an Additional Pension even if you are not entitled to the Basic Pension.

From 1978 to April 2002, Additional Pension was built up under the State Earnings-Related Pension Scheme (SERPS) but from April 2002 the State Second Pension (S2P) has replaced SERPS. Employees pay into S2P unless they are 'contracted out' of the scheme as explained below. The Additional Pension does not apply to self-employed people.

The Additional Pension is related to weekly earnings from April 1978 until the 5th of the April before your 60th (women) or 65th (men) birthday. Under the new S2P 'earnings' can also include credited earnings, as explained below. Earnings from past years (other than the one before the year you reach pension age) are revalued in line with increases in average earnings. The pension is based on each year's revalued earnings between certain levels which are known as the 'Lower and Upper Earnings Limits'. In 2002–2003 these weekly limits are £75 and £585 respectively.

If you reached pension age before 6 April 1999, your total revalued earnings have been divided by 80 to give the yearly amount of Additional Pension. This formula provides a pension based on 25 per cent of earnings between the specified levels. However, changes were introduced to phase in, between 1999 and 2009, reductions to the amount of Additional Pension people receive. The main aim of these changes was to reduce the maximum level of SERPS from 25 per cent of earnings to 20 per cent for people reaching pension age from 2009 onwards (with some protection for years up to 1987–1988). However, under S2P the amount of Additional Pension someone earns is calculated in a different way. Until changes are made to make S2P into a flat-rate pension (which will probably not be for at least five years), everyone paying into S2P will be building up at least as much pension as under SERPS and anyone earning less than around £24,000 will be building up a higher pension than under SERPS.

For further details see social security guide NP 46.

State Second Pension (S2P)

SERPS has been replaced by the State Second Pension for contributions made from April 2002. Like SERPS it is an earnings-related scheme (although it may move to a flat-rate pension in the future) but it provides extra pension to certain carers, disabled people and low-paid workers. For this tax year, 2002–2003, employees with annual earnings of at least £3,900 but less than £10,800 will be credited into the pension as though they have earnings of £10,800. You will also be treated as though you have earnings of £10,800 if, throughout the year, you are entitled to Invalid Care Allowance, or the long-term rate of Incapacity Benefit or Severe Disablement Allowance (credits for those receiving disability benefits are subject to having made a certain number of years of contributions on retirement), or you are entitled to Home Responsibilities Protection (HRP – see pages 10–12) because you are looking after a disabled person or a child under the age of six. In most cases people will be credited into S2P automatically although some people need to claim HRP and in this case from 2002–2003 you must do this by the end of the third year following the year for which you are claiming HRP.

People who have already reached pension age when the new scheme is introduced will not be affected. Those reaching pension age after April 2002 may have an Additional Pension built up partly under SERPS and partly under the State Second Pension.

Contracting out of S2P

Instead of paying into S2P (previously SERPS), people can join a 'contracted-out' occupational scheme (if their employer runs one) or take out an 'appropriate personal pension' or stakeholder pension.

If you join an employer's contracted-out occupational pension scheme, this will provide an occupational pension in place of the Additional Pension and both you and your employer will pay lower NI contributions. If you join an occupational scheme which is not contracted out, both you and your employer will pay the full-rate NI contributions and you will receive both the full Additional Pension and any pension you are due under the rules of the occupational scheme. An adjustment may be made to your occupational pension in respect of your Additional Pension. Contact the administrator of your scheme for more information. If you join an appropriate personal pension scheme or a stakeholder pension, the Inland Revenue makes a contribution direct to your pension provider.

Contracted-out occupational pension schemes, appropriate personal pension schemes and stakeholder pensions have to satisfy certain conditions.

It is a good idea to seek professional financial advice before contracting out of S2P, especially if you are considering entering a money-purchase scheme or taking out an appropriate personal pension. It is important that you continue to review your pension arrangements on a regular basis to ensure that you are making adequate provision. Again, you should take advice.

For more information about different pensions see the Age Concern Books annual publication *The Pensions Handbook*, details of which are on page 158.

For years from April 1978 to April 1997, when you receive details of your State Pension at State retirement age, this will show how much the Additional Pension would be based on your earnings. If you were contracted out of SERPS for any time, the statement will show a 'contracted-out deduction' which takes into account the time when you were not paying into SERPS. The amount of Additional Pension (before the deduction) minus the contracted-out deduction shows how much Additional Pension will actually be paid on top of your State Basic Pension.

For Additional Pension earned from April 1997, the details of your State Pension will no longer show a contracted-out deduction. For any given period of time when you were working, you will earn either Additional Pension or an occupational, personal or stakeholder pension.

Widows and widowers

When a widow starts to receive her Retirement Pension at 60, or if she is already receiving her pension at the time she is widowed, she can inherit all or some of her husband's Additional Pension (adjusted for periods when he was contracted out of SERPS/S2P). As a widow any amount you are entitled to is added to any Additional Pension on your own contributions up to the maximum amount of Additional Pension a single person could receive. Subject to this maximum level, the amount of SERPS you can inherit depends on when your husband dies and when he reaches, or was due to reach, pension age (65). You will be able to inherit all of your husband's SERPS if he dies on or before 5 October 2002, or if he dies after that date but was born on or before 5 October 1937 (and therefore reaches pension age on or before 5 October 2002).

If your husband's date of birth is between 6 October 1937 and 5 October 1945, you will be able to inherit between 60% and 90% of his SERPS depending on his precise date of birth. If he is due to reach pension age on or after 6 April 2010, you will only be able to inherit 50% of his SERPS.

Similar rules apply to a widower if both he and his wife are over pension age when she dies. In this case the husband can inherit some or all of his wife's SERPS depending on when she reaches pension age (60). He will be able to inherit all his wife's SERPS (subject to the maximum level) if she dies on or before 5 October 2002, or if she dies after that date but had already reached pension age by 5 October 2002. If a man was widowed on or after 8 April 2001, in some circumstances he may be able to inherit his wife's SERPS if he is under pension age when she dies.

As explained earlier, for contributions made from April 2002 SERPS is being replaced by the State Second Pension (S2P). The maximum amount of S2P that a widow or widower will be able to inherit is 50%, regardless of when they are widowed.

Social security guide NP 46 gives more details about how Additional Pension is calculated including information about pension rights for widows and widowers whose spouse was contracted out of SERPS/S2P. Leaflet SERPS L1 provides information about inheritance of SERPS.

GRADUATED PENSION

This taxable pension scheme existed from April 1961 to April 1975 and was based on graduated contributions paid from earnings. If you were over 18 during this period and paying graduated contributions, your Graduated Pension (also known as Graduated Retirement Benefit) for the year 2002–2003 will be based on these weekly rates:

| Women | 9.21p for every £9.00 contributions paid |
| Men | 9.21p for every £7.50 contributions paid |

This will be paid when you claim your pension, normally with the Basic Pension. However, you can receive Graduated Pension even if you do not qualify for a Basic Pension.

Married women, widows and widowers

If you are a married woman of 60 or over and your husband has put off drawing his pension, you should be aware that any Graduated Pension you receive – however little – may mean that you will not benefit from an increased married woman's pension when your husband draws his pension. See page 23 for further information.

A widow can inherit half her late husband's Graduated Pension, as can a widower whose wife died after 5 April 1979, provided they were both over pension age (60 for women, 65 for men) when she died.

OVER-80s PENSION

This is a non-contributory taxable Retirement Pension of £45.20 a week for people aged 80 or over who have no Retirement Pension. For someone who already gets a Retirement Pension of less than £45.20 a week, an Over-80s Pension will be paid to bring that pension up to this level.

To qualify for this pension you have to be living in the UK on the day you became 80 or the date of your claim if this is later, and to have been here for ten years or more in any 20-year period after your 60th birthday. If you have lived in Gibraltar or another European Union country, this may help you satisfy the conditions.

The Over-80s Pension will be counted as income in full for the purposes of Income Support (Minimum Income Guarantee), Housing Benefit and Council Tax Benefit.

See social security claim form (with notes) BR 2488.

GOING ON WORKING

This section looks at the choices open to people who wish to work after reaching pension age (60 for women, 65 for men). People can choose to claim their pension or to defer it (that is, put off drawing it) in order to gain increases later on.

Working and drawing the State Pension

Once you reach pension age, you can draw your State Pension if you satisfy the contribution conditions. It will not be affected by the amount you earn or the number of hours you work. You should note, however, that if you are claiming an addition with your pension for a dependent husband or wife, this addition could be affected by their earnings, as explained on pages 4–5.

Although your pension will not be reduced because you are working, it is counted as part of your taxable income. Your tax code will be adjusted to take into account the amount of any pension (including Additional and Graduated) you receive.

If you carry on working after pension age, you will not have to pay NI contributions. You should receive a certificate of exception from the DWP to give to your employer, who will still have to pay contributions for you.

Deferring your pension

You can choose to defer (postpone) drawing your pension for up to five years after pension age in order to earn extra pension.

You cannot normally defer a pension after the age of 65 (women) or 70 (men). However, you may be able to do so if you are a married woman of 65 or over with a husband under 70 who is deferring his pension, as explained below.

You do not have to be working to defer your pension but you will not be counted as deferring your pension if you are receiving certain other benefits instead. For example, a woman who decides not to draw her pension at the age of 60 but to continue to claim Widow's Pension until the age of 65 will not gain any extra pension. You should also note that if you are entitled to an increase for a dependant (for example because you are a married man with a wife aged under 60), this part of your pension will not be increased by deferring your pension.

Even if you start drawing your pension, it is possible to change your mind and defer it instead. However, this can only be done once. If you are a married man and your wife is drawing a pension based on your contributions, you may need your wife's consent before cancelling your pension as she will have to give hers up too.

Extra Basic Pension

If you defer your pension, it will be increased by about 7.5 per cent a year for each full year that you do not draw it. (If you were deferring your pension before 6 April 1979, you will have earned a smaller increase.) For each week that you defer your pension, it will be increased by 1/7p in the pound, but you must defer it for at least seven weeks to gain any increase.

If you put off drawing your pension for the full five years, it will be increased by about 37.5 per cent. For example, in April 2002, the Basic Pension of £75.50 a week would be increased to about £104 a week for someone who had deferred it for five years.

See social security guide NP 46 and Age Concern Factsheet 19 *The State Pension*.

Extra Additional and Graduated Pension

If you defer drawing your pension, your Additional and Graduated Pensions will be increased in the same way as the Basic Pension.

See social security guide NP 46 for information about the effect of deferring your pension on an occupational pension.

Extra pension for married women

If you are a married woman entitled to a pension on your own contributions and you defer drawing it, the pension will be increased as described previously.

If you are aged 60–64 and entitled to a pension on your husband's contributions, you can defer this to gain an increase. If you are 60 or over and your husband is deferring his pension, you will not be able to draw the married woman's pension. Once he draws his pension, you will both receive increases.

However, your pension on your husband's contributions will not be increased if, while your husband is deferring his pension, you draw another benefit such as Additional Pension or Graduated Pension. It may be better not to draw, for example, a small Additional Pension if your husband is deferring his pension.

Unemployment and sickness

If you have deferred your Retirement Pension, you cannot claim Incapacity Benefit or Jobseeker's Allowance if you become unable to work. This is because neither of these benefits can start to be paid to someone who has reached pension age.

EARLY RETIREMENT AND UNEMPLOYMENT

This section summarises the benefits available to older people who are not in work before State Pension age (60 for women, 65 for men) and explains how to ensure that your Retirement Pension is protected.

Jobseeker's Allowance (JSA)

JSA is a taxable benefit for people who are unemployed. There are two elements: contribution-based JSA, which is based on your NI contribution record, and income-based JSA, which is means-tested.

To qualify for JSA you must be:

- under pension age (although if you are aged 60–64 you can claim Income Support instead of income-based JSA);
- unemployed or working for less than 16 hours a week;
- capable of and available for work; and
- actively seeking work. You must have entered into a Jobseeker's Agreement, and you must comply with any directions given.

Contribution-based JSA can be paid for a maximum of 26 weeks. The rate for people aged 25 or over is £53.95. There are no additions for dependants. Although in general income and savings are not taken into account, if you have an occupational or personal pension of over £50 a week this will reduce any contribution-based JSA by the amount by which your pension exceeds £50.

Income-based JSA can be paid in addition to the contribution-based JSA or on its own if you do not have sufficient NI contributions or you have already received contribution-based JSA for 26 weeks. To qualify for income-based JSA you must have no more than £8,000 savings (£12,000 if you are aged 60 or over) and a low income. If you have a partner, his or her income and savings will be added to yours and your partner must either not be in work or be working for less than 24 hours a week on average. Couples may be required to make a joint claim and both partners may need to be actively seeking work and have entered into a Jobseeker's Agreement. However, if your partner is over 60 or cannot work, for example because they are disabled or a carer, or if they are working at least 16 hours a week but less than 24, they will not have to meet the jobseeking requirements.

The rules for calculating income-based JSA are similar to those for Income Support described on pages 41–51. If you qualify for income-based JSA you may also get other benefits such as Housing Benefit and Council Tax Benefit and help with NHS costs. If you do not have to sign on in order to receive benefit (for example because you are aged 60 or over or are a carer receiving Invalid Care Allowance) then you can claim Income Support instead of income-based JSA.

How to claim

You claim JSA from your local Jobcentre Plus office, where you will be given a claim pack and an interview will be arranged. You will need to complete a claim form which covers information needed to check your entitlement to benefit and details of the type of work you are looking for. At your interview an adviser should discuss benefits and other support as well as covering employment options. At the end of the interview you will have to sign a Jobseeker's Agreement which outlines the action you are expected to take to find work. Once JSA is awarded, you will need to attend your local office every two weeks.

In some situations benefit may be stopped for a limited period. For example, if you leave work voluntarily without 'good cause' or refuse a job, then you may lose benefit for up to 26 weeks. You may lose benefit if you accept early retirement, although not if you are made redundant.

If you are refused benefit or need more information or help or advice with claiming JSA, contact a local advice agency.

Schemes to help people back to work

The Government's 'New Deal' programme aims to help people into work. It includes the New Deal for Disabled People and the New Deal for Long-Term Unemployed. There is also a 'New Deal for over 50's'. Under the scheme people are offered assistance from a personal adviser, job search support and an in-work training subsidy. There is also a cash employment credit of £60 for up to a year for people entering full-time work (£40 for part-time) who have been out of work and on benefits for six months or more. In 2003 a new scheme, the Working Tax Credit, is due to be introduced. This tax credit will provide financial support to people in work who are living in low income households. It is planned that this will include an additional element for older workers, paid for a limited time, which will replace the current New Deal 50 Plus Employment Credit.

Two other measures to encourage people to work are the 'Back to work bonus' and the continuation of Housing Benefit and Council Tax Benefit for an extra four weeks after you start work and your JSA stops. The Government is also looking at other ways to encourage people to move from benefits to work.

Ask at the Jobcentre for further information.

Incapacity Benefit

If you are unable to work because of sickness and are no longer employed, you may be entitled to Incapacity Benefit, depending on your contribution record. See pages 96–101 for details.

Occupational and personal pensions

You may qualify for some occupational pension before pension age (60 for women, 65 for men) if you retire early. You should check with your employer for details.

You can usually draw a personal pension or stakeholder pension at any time between the ages of 50 and 75. However, if you were contracted out of SERPS/S2P, you cannot start to receive the part of your personal or stakeholder pension built up from the minimum NI contributions paid into your fund until you reach the age of 60.

Income-related benefits

In addition to the types of income described above, such as Incapacity Benefit and occupational pensions, you may be able to receive one or more of the income-related benefits – Income Support, income-based Jobseeker's Allowance, Housing Benefit and Council Tax Benefit. These benefits depend on your income, savings and other factors. Income Support and Jobseeker's Allowance cannot be paid together. You can receive Income Support only if you do not need to 'sign on' for work in order to receive benefit.

Protecting your State Pension

To make sure that you have paid enough contributions to receive a full pension when you reach pension age, check your contribution record by contacting your local social security office.

You will receive credits towards your pension if you are drawing a benefit such as Jobseeker's Allowance or Incapacity Benefit. If you are under 60 and seeking work, it may be worth signing on as unemployed – even if you are not entitled to benefit – because you will receive credits. If you are a man aged 60–64, you will normally receive credits automatically even if you are not ill or signing on as unemployed. However, you cannot get these automatic credits for any tax year during which you are abroad for more than six months. If you are not entitled to credits and have an incomplete NI record, you may want to consider paying voluntary contributions.

BEREAVEMENT BENEFITS

This section covers the bereavement benefits that men and women widowed before pension age may be entitled to. It does not cover the position for people with dependent children who should seek further information from a local advice agency.

People widowed on or after 9 April 2001 may be entitled to the Bereavement Payment and the Bereavement Allowance. These apply to both men and women and are based on their late spouse's contribution record. Before April 2001 benefits were only given to widows. When you register the death the Registrar will give you a form to send to the social security office in order to claim these benefits.

Women widowed before 9 April 2001 may be receiving Widow's Pension. People widowed after pension age may be entitled to claim a State Pension based on their late husband's or wife's contributions, as explained on pages 6–7.

Bereavement Payment

The Bereavement Payment was introduced on 9 April 2001 and is a single lump-sum payment of £2,000. It is tax free and is paid mainly to widows and widowers under pension age. If you are over pension age when your spouse dies, you will still receive the payment provided that your spouse was under pension age or was over pension age (60 for women, 65 for men) but not receiving a State Retirement Pension based on his or her own contribution record.

The Bereavement Payment replaced the Widow's Payment which started in April 1988 and was a £1,000 payment made only to widows (mainly those under the age of 60).

Bereavement Allowance

The Bereavement Allowance replaced the Widow's Pension for people widowed on or after 9 April 2001. It is paid to both men and women who are aged at least 45 but under pension age when they are widowed and whose spouse fulfilled the contribution conditions. The full rate is £75.50 but you will get less if you were widowed before the age of 55. (You cannot receive any of your spouse's State Additional Pension.) It will be paid for a maximum of 52 weeks but will stop sooner if you remarry or reach pension age during that period. Once you reach pension age you may be able to claim a State Retirement Pension based on your late husband's or wife's contributions, as explained on pages 6–7.

If you claim Income Support or Jobseeker's Allowance, when the Bereavement Allowance ends you may receive extra help through the bereavement premium (provided that you were 55 or over but under 60 on 9 April 2001 and widowed before April 2006), as explained on page 49.

Widow's Pension

If your husband died before 9 April 2001, you may be in receipt of a Widow's Pension and this will not have been affected by the introduction of the new bereavement benefits. The full standard rate is £75.50 but you may be getting less if you were under 55 when you were widowed or if your husband did not have a full contribution record. You may also be receiving an Additional Pension based on your husband's earnings since 1978, taking into account any periods that he was contracted out of SERPS.

When you reach pension age (60), you can draw the State Retirement Pension instead of the Widow's Pension or you can remain on the Widow's Pension until you reach 65. The amounts will often be the same, but you may also receive some Graduated Pension with the State Pension. Check with the DWP what the different amounts would be.

The Widow's Pension will not be affected by your earnings. However, if you do not draw your Retirement Pension at the age of 60, you will not earn extra pension unless you give up the Widow's Pension.

If you remarry before you reach 60, you will lose the Widow's Pension. It will also be suspended during any period when you live with a man as his wife. However, if you are 60 or over and receive a Retirement Pension based on your previous husband's contributions, you will not lose this if you remarry or live with someone.

See social security guide NP 45 and leaflet BERE *New Bereavement Benefits*.

CHRISTMAS BONUS

The Christmas Bonus of £10 will be paid to people who are entitled to one of the State benefits listed below and who are living in the UK or any European Union country during the week beginning 2 December 2002. The bonus is tax-free and has no effect on other benefits.

Who qualifies?

You will get the Christmas Bonus if you are receiving a Retirement Pension; Over-80s or Widow's Pension; Attendance Allowance; Disability Living Allowance (any level or component); Invalid Care Allowance; Industrial Death Benefit; Incapacity Benefit payable at the long-term rate; Severe Disablement Allowance; Income Support (provided you have reached pension age: 60 for women, 65 for men); War Widow's Pension; Unemployability Supplement or Allowance; or Constant Attendance Allowance paid with a War or Industrial Disablement Pension. It is also payable to someone aged 65 or over who receives a War Disablement Pension, but who does not get a qualifying social security benefit.

Only one bonus can be given to each person. However, someone over pension age may get an additional bonus for a dependent spouse or an unmarried partner who is over pension age or who reaches pension age during the week beginning 2 December 2002 but is not entitled to the bonus in their own right, as long as the relevant conditions are satisfied.

How it is paid

There is usually no need to claim, as the bonus is paid automatically. Depending on the way your pension is normally paid, the bonus will be added to your pension to collect at the post office, paid into a bank or building society account, or sent by giro cheque. If you think you are entitled to the bonus but do not receive it by the end of December, inform your local social security office.

DECISION MAKING AND APPEALS

This section outlines the system of decision making and the way that you can challenge a decision about a State Pension or benefit. There is a different review system for the discretionary Social Fund, which is explained on page 61.

When you receive a letter giving details of whether you have been awarded a benefit, and if so how much, you will also get information about what to do if you disagree with the decision. It is very important to be aware that there are time limits for challenging decisions and you should take action as soon as possible if you are unhappy with a decision.

If you want to challenge a decision it is often useful to get advice from a local agency such as a Citizens Advice Bureau. For example they may be able to advise on whether you have a good case; contact the social security office on your behalf; prepare your case; and they may perhaps be able to represent you at an appeal tribunal.

Decisions

Most social security decisions are made by the Secretary of State – in practice by a decision maker in the social security office on behalf of the Secretary of State. Decisions on Housing and Council Tax Benefit are made by decision makers in the local authority. In most situations decisions can be revised or superseded or you can take the matter to an appeal tribunal. However you should note that the information below does not apply to certain types of decision such as how benefits are paid. These decisions are not subject to the appeals procedures although you can still ask for the decision to be reconsidered. For some decisions about contributions you will need to contact the Inland Revenue if you disagree with the decision.

Revising and superseding decisions

If you are refused benefit or disagree with the amount awarded you have one calendar month to ask for the decision to be revised (ie to be looked at again and changed). If you have not been given a written 'statement of reasons' for the decision, you can ask for one, in which case the time limit will be extended by 14 days. The one month time limit can also be extended to up to 13 months in certain situations if there are 'special circumstances' for asking for a late revision. If you are asking for the decision to be revised you should send in any additional information that might help. Asking for a revision is intended to be a quick and flexible procedure. You can do this by letter or telephone, explaining why you think the decision is wrong – you should make it clear that you are asking for your benefit to be revised. You will then be sent a letter explaining whether the decision is being revised and if you are still not happy with the decision you can appeal.

Decisions awarding benefit may also be 'superseded' at any time if, for example, your circumstances change or there is new information which affects the decision. You should let the social security office know as soon as possible about any information that might affect your benefit. Otherwise you may lose benefit or receive too much and have to repay money.

Appeals

If you have asked for a decision to be revised, and you are not happy with the outcome, you can appeal. You should appeal within one month of the date on the letter about the revision although this time can be extended to up to 13 months if your appeal has a reasonable prospect of success and there are 'special circumstances' why it is late. You can also appeal straightaway without asking for a revision – again this must normally be done within one month. If you appeal, the decision will be looked at again to see if it can be revised. If the decision is revised in your favour the appeal will not go ahead, even if you do not get all you asked for in the appeal. You can appeal against the new decision if you are still unhappy. You should ask for an appeal using the form attached to leaflet GL 24 if possible (although other requests in writing may be accepted), saying which decision you are appealing against and giving the reasons why you disagree with the decision.

Although most appeals will be considered by a tribunal, there will be the option for the Appeals Service to 'strike out' an appeal, for example if it is considered to be 'misconceived' or if you do not provide information requested within the specified time limits. Contact a local agency for help if this happens. When your appeal is accepted you will be sent information and papers relevant to your case. You must let the Appeals Service know if you wish to attend the tribunal or if you want the decision to be made just on the basis of the written information you have provided. It is always better to attend if possible so as to have an opportunity to explain the position and answer questions.

Tribunals

Appeals are administered by the Appeals Service, a Department for Work and Pensions (DWP) agency. Tribunals will consist of one, two or three people depending on the benefit involved and the issues raised. Tribunal members are independent of the DWP and one will be a lawyer. There will also usually be an officer from the social security office present.

When you arrive at the tribunal, a clerk will explain the procedures, which are intended to be as informal as possible. You will be given time to put your case and the tribunal will ask questions. The clerk should reimburse your travel expenses before you leave. The tribunal must decide whether the decision was right according to the law, but cannot change a decision just because it seems unfair. You may be told the outcome straightaway; otherwise notification of the decision will be sent to you later.

If you are unhappy with the tribunal's decision, you may be able to make a further appeal to a Social Security Commissioner; you should seek advice from a local advice agency about how to do this.

For more detailed information see social security guide NI 260 DMA or the CPAG's *Welfare Benefits Handbook* (see page 155).

OCCUPATIONAL AND PERSONAL PENSIONS

This section gives brief information about occupational, personal and stakeholder pensions and sources of advice if you have a problem. It also summarises how these pensions can affect your State benefits.

Occupational pensions are run by employers and are also known as 'company' pensions or, for public sector workers, 'superannuation'. Personal pensions and the new stakeholder pensions are provided by financial institutions, such as banks, building societies and insurance companies. Employees earning over a certain level must either be paying into the State Additional Pension or be contracted-out into an occupational, personal or stakeholder pension, as explained on pages 17–19. Self-employed people do not have access to occupational pension schemes but can take out personal pensions or stakeholder pensions. Stakeholder pensions have been available since April 2001 and must satisfy certain government standards with the aim of providing flexibility and value for money.

It is not within the scope of this book to give information about the different types of pension scheme, and in any case terms and conditions vary. You should therefore contact your scheme provider for more information – for example if you need to find out more about provision for widows or other dependants. (If you have paid into one or more pensions in the past you may be able to trace the scheme through the Pension Schemes Registry, PO Box 1NN, Newcastle Upon Tyne NE99 1NN. Tel: 0191 225 6316.)

Getting advice

If you have a problem relating to your pension that you cannot sort out with your employer or pension provider, you can contact the Pensions Advisory Service (OPAS – address on page 154) or a Citizens Advice Bureau. OPAS is an independent voluntary organisation with a network of local advisers who can offer free help and advice. If OPAS cannot resolve your problem, it may suggest that you make a complaint to the Pensions Ombudsman, or to the Insurance Ombudsman Bureau in the case of a personal pension.

See Age Concern Books annual publication *The Pensions Handbook* for further information about different types of pension. The Department for Work and Pensions produces a number of leaflets on State Pensions and other pensions – these can be obtained from the Pensions Info-Line on 0845 731 3233. The OPAS Pensions Helpline on 0845 601 2923 can provide impartial information and guidance but not specific financial advice.

How State benefits are affected

An occupational, personal or stakeholder pension will be counted as income in full for the purposes of benefits such as Income Support, income-based Jobseeker's Allowance (JSA), Housing Benefit and Council Tax Benefit. It can also reduce the amount of contribution-based JSA you get (see page 24) or the amount of Incapacity Benefit paid (see page 98). If you receive a pension or benefit and wish to claim an increase for a dependent wife or husband, any occupational, personal or stakeholder pension they receive will be counted as earnings and may affect your increase, as explained on pages 4–5.

Income-Related (Means-Tested) Benefits

This part of Your Rights *describes benefits that older people may be able to claim depending on their income and savings. It covers Income Support (Minimum Income Guarantee), Housing Benefit and Council Tax Benefit, which help with regular weekly expenses, and the Discretionary Social Fund, which provides lump-sum payments for exceptional expenses. Income-based Jobseeker's Allowance, which is paid to unemployed people under pension age, is not described, but it is calculated in a similar way to Income Support.*

Many older people are entitled to these benefits but do not make a claim, so it is important to check your position to make sure that you are not missing out on income that is due to you.

In 2003 a new Pension Credit will replace Income Support and provide extra cash to people who have saved. At the same time changes will be made to the assessment of capital for Housing and Council Tax Benefit – see pages 56–57 for more information.

INCOME SUPPORT (MINIMUM INCOME GUARANTEE)

Throughout this book we refer to 'Income Support' but you should be aware that the Government and others describe Income Support for people aged 60 and over as the 'Minimum Income Guarantee' or MIG. If you are already receiving Income Support you cannot get anything extra by applying for the Minimum Income Guarantee because it is the same thing.

Income Support is a benefit which helps with weekly basic living expenses by topping up your income to a level set by the Government. You do not need to have paid National Insurance (NI) contributions to qualify for Income Support, but your income and any savings and capital over a certain level will be taken into account. Income Support is not taxable.

If you receive Income Support, you are also likely to qualify for Housing Benefit and/or Council Tax Benefit, which are based on similar rules. These benefits help with rent and Council Tax payments. If your income or savings are too high for you to qualify for Income Support, you may still be entitled to Housing Benefit and Council Tax Benefit.

Income Support can be paid to homeowners, tenants, and people in other circumstances such as living with family or friends. Once you get Income Support, you may also get other benefits such as help towards glasses (see page 134), free dental treatment (see page 133) and possibly lump-sum payments from the Social Fund (see pages 58–61).

See leaflet MIG 1L *Minimum Income Guarantee* or social security guide IS 20 for detailed information.

Who qualifies?

You may receive Income Support if you fulfil all the following conditions:

- Your savings are £12,000 or less if you are aged 60 or over (£16,000 if you live in a care home or £8,000 if you are aged under 60).
- You have a low income.
- You are aged 60 or over or you are under 60 but do not need to 'sign on' as unemployed, for example because you are ill or you are a carer. Unemployed people receive income-based Jobseeker's Allowance instead (see pages 24–25).
- You do not work 16 hours a week or more and your partner (if you have one) does not work 24 hours a week or more.
- You are habitually resident in the UK and you are not excluded from claiming benefit because of your immigration status. Contact a local advice agency if you need further advice about the benefit position for people who have been living abroad.

A 'partner' is your husband or wife or someone of the opposite sex who you live with as though you were married. Throughout this section the word 'partner' will be used instead of 'spouse' because you do not have to be married to be treated as a couple. You apply for Income Support for yourself and your partner. If you live with someone else such as a friend, you can both apply for Income Support separately.

How to work it out

Income Support is worked out by using the following steps, which are explained below:

1 Add up the value of your savings, but note that certain types of savings are ignored.
2 Add up your weekly income, but note that certain kinds of income are ignored.
3 Work out the amount the Government says you need to live on, called the 'applicable amount'.
4 Compare your applicable amount with your income to see whether you are entitled to benefit.

1 Your savings

Throughout this book the term 'savings' is used to cover savings, capital, investments and property.

In April 2001 the savings limits increased for people aged 60 or over so that the limits are now higher than those for younger people. For a couple, only one of you needs to be 60 or over to get the higher levels. This book is aimed mainly at people aged 60 or over, but the differences for younger people are referred to.

If your savings are more than £12,000 (£8,000 for people aged under 60), you cannot get Income Support. For a couple, savings are added together, but the limit is the same. Different savings limits apply to people claiming Income Support in care homes, as explained on page 125.

If you have savings of between £6,000 and £12,000 (£3,000 and £8,000 for people aged under 60), an income of £1 a week for every £250 (or part of £250) over £6,000 (or £3,000) will be taken into account when working out your benefit. For example, a 70-year old with savings of £6,480 will be treated as having an income of £2 a week; savings of £8,760 will be treated as £12 a week. This is called 'tariff income'. Savings of £6,000 (£3,000 if you are under 60) or less will not affect your benefit.

● **If you 'deprive' yourself of savings in order to get benefit or to increase the amount of benefit, you will be considered as still having those savings. Depriving yourself of savings might include giving money to your family or buying expensive items in order to gain benefit. You should seek advice if you are refused benefit because of this.**

Savings and capital are normally valued at their current market or surrender value. If there are expenses involved in selling them, 10 per cent will be deducted. Most forms of savings and capital will be taken into account, including:

- cash;
- bank and building society accounts (including current accounts that do not pay interest);
- National Savings accounts and certificates (valued according to rules which the local social security office will explain);
- premium bonds;
- stocks and shares;
- property; and
- a share of any savings you own jointly with other people – these will be divided equally by the number of joint owners to calculate your share.

Some types of savings will be ignored, including:

- the value of your home if you own it and are living there;
- the surrender value of a life assurance policy (although if a policy is cashed in the money you receive will normally be counted);
- arrears of certain benefits such as Attendance Allowance, Disability Living Allowance or Income Support for 52 weeks from the date you receive them;
- your personal possessions, unless they have been bought in order to reduce your savings; and
- the £10,000 ex-gratia payment for Far Eastern Prisoners of War (see page 107).

Your money should not normally be counted as both 'income' and 'savings'. So if, for example, your pension is paid four-weekly into a bank account, this should not be assessed as part of your savings unless it is still unspent at the end of the four-week period.

2 Your income

Income includes earnings, State pensions and benefits, occupational, personal or stakeholder pensions and any other money you have coming in after tax and NI contributions have been paid. For a couple, the income of both partners is added together when calculating Income Support.

However, some income may be fully or **partly** ignored when your benefit is calculated. Income that will be fully ignored includes:

- Housing Benefit and Council Tax Benefit;
- the mobility component of Disability Living Allowance;
- Attendance Allowance and the care component of Disability Living Allowance;
- actual interest or income from savings or capital of £12,000 (£8,000 if you are aged under 60) or less (only tariff income will be counted, as explained above). Interest is not counted as income but once it is paid into an account it will be counted as part of your savings;
- the special war widow's pension for 'pre-1973 widows', which is now £59.95 (in addition to the £10 of a War Widow's Pension outlined below); and
- payments made to you (for example by a relative or charity) for things not covered by benefit such as telephone costs, TV rental or holidays, as long as you actually use them for these purposes.

The following are examples of parts of weekly income that will also be ignored:

- £5 of your earnings if you work part-time and are single;
- £10 of your or your partner's earnings from part-time work (if you both work the maximum is still £10);
- £20 of earnings if you work part-time and you are a carer receiving the carer premium or in certain circumstances when you or your partner is disabled (instead of the £5 or £10 listed above);
- £10 of a War Widow's Pension or War Disablement Pension;
- £20 of regular payments from a friend, relative or charity, unless these are fully ignored, as described above (but this £20 will not be ignored on top of £10 from a war pension because the total amount from these two types of income that can be ignored must not be more than £20);
- £4 of any payment from a subtenant living in your home;

- £13.40 of any payment from a subtenant which includes an amount for heating; and
- £20 income from a boarder plus half of the boarder's charge over £20.

Having decided what kinds of income will be ignored, add up the rest of your income, including tariff income for savings between £6,000 and £12,000 (£3,000 and £8,000 if you are aged under 60). The total is the weekly income used to work out your Income Support.

3 Your applicable amount

This is the weekly amount intended to meet your day-to-day living needs. It is worked out by adding together the personal allowance for a single person or a couple and any premiums that apply to you. Premiums are awarded to particular groups such as those aged over 60 and disabled people. For Income Support certain housing costs for homeowners can also be included, as explained on pages 51–53. Allowances and premiums for children are not covered here. Once you have worked out your applicable amount, you will be able to check whether you are likely to qualify for one or more of the income-related benefits (Income Support, Housing Benefit and Council Tax Benefit). See pages 123–130 for more information for people living in care homes.

Personal allowances

The personal allowances for people over 25 are shown below:

Single person	£53.95
Couple	£84.65

Premiums

Premiums are part of the system of income-related benefits. You must add these to your personal allowance to see if you qualify for Income Support, Housing Benefit and/or Council Tax Benefit.

People aged 60 or over can receive a pensioner premium and may also be entitled to the carer premium or the severe disability premium if they satisfy the conditions.

Disabled people under 60 may be able to receive the disability premium and in some cases the enhanced disability premium and/or the severe disability premium as well. There is also the bereavement premium (although this cannot be awarded to people who are in receipt of the disability premium) and the carer premium which can be awarded in addition to any other premiums.

Pensioner premium (for people aged 60 and over)

Until April 2001 there were three levels of premium for people aged 60 and over – the pensioner, enhanced pensioner and higher pensioner premiums. However the amounts are now the same, whatever your age. You will qualify for the premium if you are a single person aged 60 or over, or one of a couple and either you or your partner is aged 60 or over. The rates are:

Single person	£44.20
Couple	£65.15

You should note that although there is only one level of premium, when you receive a letter explaining how your benefit is calculated, this may still refer to the 'enhanced pensioner' or 'higher pensioner' premium. Remember that some people in receipt of Attendance Allowance or Disability Living Allowance may qualify for the severe disability premium as well and some carers may get a carer premium, as explained below.

Disability premium

This is given to disabled people under 60. To be counted as 'disabled', you must normally be getting a disability benefit such as Disability Living Allowance (any level or component), Severe Disablement Allowance or the long-term rate of Incapacity Benefit or be registered as blind. For a couple, only one of you needs to fulfil these conditions. The rates are:

Single person	£23.00
Couple	£32.80

People may also be able to receive the disability premium in some situations where they have been unable to work for at least 52 weeks but do not receive one of the disability benefits listed above.

Enhanced disability premium

This premium was introduced in April 2001. It is awarded to people under the age of 60 who are in receipt of the highest level of the care component of Disability Living Allowance. It is awarded in addition to the disability premium.

Single person	£11.25
Couple	£16.25

Severe disability premium

Single people will get this provided they 'live alone' (but see below for exceptions to this) and receive Attendance Allowance or the middle or highest level of the care component of Disability Living Allowance (DLA), with no one receiving Invalid Care Allowance for looking after them. However, there are exceptions to the living alone rule: for example, you can still get this premium if you live with someone who also gets Attendance Allowance (or the middle or highest level of the care component of DLA), or with someone who is registered blind, or with a paid helper supplied by a charity, or in some cases where you are a joint tenant or joint owner and share the housing costs. If you are not sure if you qualify, seek further advice as the rules can be complicated.

If you have a partner and you receive Attendance Allowance (or the middle or highest level of the care component of DLA), you will not normally be able to receive this premium because you will not be counted as 'living alone'. However, you can receive this premium if:

- your partner also gets Attendance Allowance (or the middle or highest level of the care component of DLA) or he or she is registered blind; and

- no one receives Invalid Care Allowance for looking after
you; and
- you 'live alone' as described above.

If your partner also receives Attendance Allowance (or the
middle or highest level of the care component of DLA) and
neither of you has a carer receiving Invalid Care Allowance,
you will receive the double rate. The rates are:

Single person	£42.25
Couple, one person qualifying	£42.25
Couple, both qualifying	£84.50

- **Remember that the severe disability premium can be awarded
on top of the disability, enhanced disability and pensioner
premiums.**

Carer premium

This premium is given to carers who are receiving Invalid Care
Allowance (ICA – see pages 91–94). It will also be given to
people who applied for ICA on or after 1 October 1990 and
fulfil all the conditions but cannot receive it because they are
getting another benefit instead.

For example, if you are receiving a Widow's Pension of £75.50,
you will not be paid ICA as well. However, if you apply for
ICA, you may receive a letter saying that you are entitled to
ICA but cannot be paid it, which you can show to the social
security office (for Income Support) or the council (for Housing
and Council Tax Benefit), which will award you the premium.
At the time of writing ICA can only be awarded to people who
are aged under 65 when they apply, but the Government has
said that it will change this rule in the future.

The carer premium continues to be paid for eight weeks after
the person you care for dies, or you cease being a carer for
some other reason. The rates for the carer premium are:

Single person	£24.80
Couple, one person qualifying	£24.80
Couple, both qualifying	£49.60

- Warning: If the person you care for receives the severe disability premium (see above), they will lose this when you receive your first payment of ICA. You might be able to receive an extra £24.80 a week through the carer premium while the person you care for would lose a premium worth £42.25. If you are not sure whether to claim ICA or not, get advice first.

Bereavement premium

This premium has been introduced to provide additional support on a temporary basis to certain widows and widowers. It will end in April 2006. To qualify you must have been receiving the Bereavement Allowance (see pages 28–29) because you were widowed on or after 9 April 2001, but are no longer entitled to it. You must have been aged 55 or over but under 60 on 9 April 2001. Once you reach 60 the premium will stop and you will start to receive the pensioner premium instead which is awarded at a higher level. The bereavement premium is only available to single people (ie you will lose it if you remarry or live with someone as though you were married) and the rate is:

Single person   £21.55

4 Calculating Income Support

Once you have worked out your applicable amount by adding together your personal allowance and any premiums, compare this figure with your income. If your income is less than your applicable amount, you will qualify for Income Support (depending on your savings). If your income is the same or more, you will not get Income Support but you may get Housing Benefit and/or Council Tax Benefit.

Example

Rose Williams is aged 76, and lives alone in a council flat. Her only income is the State Pension of £75.50 a week. She has savings of £950.

Rose adds up her income

Retirement Pension	£75.50

Rose works out her applicable amount

Personal allowance	£53.95
Premium for age 60+	£44.20
Total	£98.15

Rose's income of £75.50 a week is less than her applicable amount of £98.15. The difference is £22.65. This is how much Income Support she will get on top of her Retirement Pension.

Rose will also get Housing Benefit and Council Tax Benefit to cover all her rent and Council Tax.

Example

Bill and Mary McConnell are a married couple both aged 70. Their joint State Pensions come to £120.70 and Bill gets a pension of £35 a week from his old job. They live in their own home and they have savings of £7,000. Mary suffers with rheumatoid arthritis and gets Attendance Allowance.

Bill and Mary add up their income, ignoring Mary's Attendance Allowance

State Pension	£120.70
Occupational pension	£35.00
Weekly tariff income from savings	£4.00
Total	£159.70

Bill and Mary work out their applicable amount

Personal allowance	£84.65
Premium for age 60+	£65.15
Total	£149.80

Their income is £9.90 a week more than their applicable amount, so they do not qualify for Income Support. But they should claim Council Tax Benefit to get help with their Council Tax payments.

Example

Andrew Jennings is 80 and lives alone in his own home. His State Pension is £75.75 and he has an occupational pension of £30. He has no savings. Last year he applied for Income Support but was turned down because his income was too high although he received some help from Council Tax Benefit. In October 2001 he had a stroke. He now has difficulty with getting dressed and washed but has been able to continue to live on his own with support. No one receives Invalid Care Allowance for looking after him. His local Age Concern helped him claim Attendance Allowance and advised him to reapply for Income Support.

Andrew's income, ignoring the Attendance Allowance

State Pension	£75.75
Occupational pension	£30.00
	£105.75

Andrew's applicable amount

Personal allowance	£53.95
Premium for age 60+	£44.20
Severe disability premium	£42.25
	£140.40

His income is £34.65 less than his applicable amount so he receives £34.65 Income Support and Council Tax Benefit will cover all his Council Tax.

Help with housing costs

In addition to your personal allowance and any premiums, the Income Support applicable amount can also include an additional sum for certain housing costs for those who own their property. Rent and service charges for tenants can be covered by Housing Benefit. Subject to the restrictions below, if you are aged 60 or over the housing costs which can be included are:

- mortgage Interest,
- interest on a loan for certain repairs or improvements;
- ground rent; and
- certain service charges.

If the loan is for more than £100,000 or your housing costs are considered too high (taking into account your situation), the amount added to the applicable amount may be restricted. Housing costs are paid at the start of the Income Support claim for people who are aged 60 and over. Those under 60 will have to wait for 39 weeks until help is provided towards their housing costs. Payment is only made towards the eligible mortgage interest and does not cover any payments towards arrears, capital or endowment policies. Claimants may have to meet any shortfall in payments, when their lender's interest rate is higher than the Standard Interest Rate, which is used to calculate benefit support. Payment towards eligible housing costs are generally made direct to a claimant's lender.

If you are receiving Income Support or have been receiving it within the previous 26 weeks, you may only receive help towards any new housing costs in very limited circumstances. You should seek advice before taking out a loan.

Deductions for people living in your home

The help provided towards your housing costs may be reduced if there is someone else living in your home apart from your partner or a dependent child. This is because people such as adult sons and daughters (often called 'non-dependants') are expected to contribute to housing costs. Deductions are made according to the circumstances of the non-dependant. However, no reduction will be made if you or your partner is blind or you or your partner receives Attendance Allowance or the care component of Disability Living Allowance.

There are no deductions if the person living with you is: a boarder; a full-time student; or is under 25 and receiving Income Support or income-based Jobseeker's Allowance. If the person living with you is aged 18 or over, works 16 hours a week or more, and has an income of at least £88 a week, the following deductions will be made:

Gross income of non-dependant	Weekly deduction
£88.00 to £130.99	£17.00
£131.00 to £169.99	£23.35
£170.00 to £224.99	£38.20
£225.00 to £280.99	£43.50
£281.00 or more	£47.75

For others aged 18 or over, or people aged 25 or over on Income Support or income-based Jobseeker's Allowance (JSA), the deduction will be £7.40. If there is a couple living with you, only one deduction will be made.

Example

Desmond and Marie Wilson (both aged 65) have a mortgage. Their mortgage interest is assessed as £30 a week, so their applicable amount is worked out in the following way:

Personal allowance for a couple	£84.65
Premium for age 60+	£65.15
Weekly mortgage interest	£30.00
Total	£179.80

Their daughter who is 30 and earns £140 a week comes to live with them. There will therefore be a deduction of £23.35 from the amount allowed for mortgage interest. Their total Income Support applicable amount will then be reduced to £156.45. This means that, depending on their savings, Desmond and Marie will receive Income Support if their income is less than £156.45 a week.

Income Support for people in different circumstances

Living in someone else's home

If you live in someone else's home as a member of their household – for example, with your son or daughter – Income Support will be worked out in the normal way. However, if your son or daughter gets help with housing costs through Income Support, income-based JSA, Housing Benefit or Council Tax Benefit, this may be reduced because you are living there.

Boarders and hostel dwellers

If you are living in a hotel, guest house or hostel, or in board and lodgings, Income Support will be worked out in the normal way. You can claim Housing Benefit towards the rental element of your charges and some services. You will have to pay for meals, fuel and other items that are not covered by Housing Benefit from your weekly Income Support.

If you go into hospital

If you receive the severe disability premium your Income Support will usually be reduced after four weeks in hospital. Otherwise Income Support is normally reduced after six weeks if either you or your partner goes into hospital. (This is expected to be increased to 13 weeks in October 2003 with the new Pension Credit.)

If you are single, your personal allowance will reduce to £18.90 a week after you have been in hospital for six weeks. You will not get any premiums, but you will still get housing costs. If you have a partner, your personal allowance will reduce by £15.10 a week after either you or your partner has been in hospital for six weeks. If your Income Support stops you may still receive some Housing and/or Council Tax Benefit but you will need to apply to the local authority.

After 52 weeks in hospital, a single person will have an applicable amount of £15.10 but no housing costs. If you have a partner, your personal allowance will be £15.10 and he or she will be assessed separately.

Let the social security office know about an admission to hospital, and, if your Income Support has been reduced or stopped, make sure that you tell them when you go home.

Care homes

Income Support for people in care homes is generally calculated as described here but see pages 125–126 for the differences.

How to claim Income Support

You can obtain a claim form from the local social security office by calling in, writing or telephoning or you can ring the Minimum Income Guarantee helpline on 0800 028 11 11. Staff on this number can help you fill in the form over the phone or you can ask for help at the local social security office, Citizens Advice Bureau or welfare rights advice agency. The claim form for people aged 60 and over has been shortened to ten pages to make claiming easier.

Income Support can be backdated for up to three months in certain specified circumstances when it is reasonable for you not to have claimed earlier. Once you are receiving Income Support you should let the social security office know of any changes in your circumstances that might affect your benefit.

Income Support and the Retirement Pension are normally paid together. If you collect your pension weekly at the post office, your Income Support will be paid with the pension. If you prefer, you can choose to have both paid weekly directly into a bank or building society account.

If you disagree with a decision

If you disagree with a decision that has been made about your Income Support (for example you may have been refused a premium), you can ask for the decision to be revised or appeal against the decision (see pages 32–35). You also have the right to ask for more detailed information about why a decision was made.

Pension Credit

The Pension Credit is due to be introduced in October 2003 and will provide additional cash to people who have saved. A summary of how it is expected to work is given here. It will consist of two parts – the 'guarantee credit' and the 'savings credit'.

The guarantee credit will replace Income Support for people aged 60 or over (the Minimum Income Guarantee). Like Income Support, the guarantee credit will top someone's income up to a set amount which is expected to be around £100 for a single person and £154 for a couple in 2003. There will also be extra amounts for severely disabled people and carers in line with the current system.

The savings credit, which will be available to people aged 65 and over, will provide extra cash to those who have income of more than the level of the 'savings credit threshold', which is expected to be around the level of the Basic State Pension in 2003. It will therefore help people on modest incomes who have income in addition to the Basic State Pension such as occupational pensions, the State Additional Pension, or income from savings.

People with income of more than the Basic Pension (expected to be around £77 for a single person and £123 for a couple in 2003), but less than the guarantee level, will receive an additional 60 pence for every £1 over the Basic Pension level. People with income above the guarantee level may also benefit from the savings credit. Single people with income of between

£100 and £134 are expected to receive between a maximum of £13.80 and a minimum of 20 pence, while couples with incomes of between £134 and £200 will gain between £18.60 and a minimum of 20 pence.

As with the current system the first £6,000 of savings will be ignored, but the upper limit will be removed. Currently savings of above £6,000 are assumed to produce an income of £1 for every £250 – equivalent of a return of about 20% – but under the new system this will be changed so that the assumed return will be around 10%. The new system of assumed income will also apply to Housing and Council Tax Benefit for people aged 60 or over but for these benefits the £16,000 upper limit will be retained except for those entitled to the guarantee credit.

There will also be administrative changes – for example it is expected that for most people aged 65 and over a claim will normally last for five years. Their circumstances will be reviewed at the end of this period. During this period only major changes will need to be notified, although people will be able to request a reassessment if their entitlement is likely to have gone up. These changes are also expected to apply from April 2003 to Housing Benefit and Council Tax Benefit claims for people aged 65 and over.

At the time of writing Parliament was still considering the proposals, so there may be changes. For more information contact Age Concern England at the address on page 157 or ring Freephone 0800 00 99 66.

THE SOCIAL FUND

The Social Fund provides lump-sum payments for expenses which are difficult to meet from low income. There are Funeral Payments, which are described on pages 141–142, and Cold Weather Payments, which are explained on page 113. In addition there are Winter Fuel Payments which are not related to income (see pages 112–113). If you have other expenses, for example if you need a cooker or bedding, you may get help from the discretionary Social Fund in the form of Community Care Grants, Budgeting Loans or Crisis Loans which are covered in this section.

The payments described here are different from most other social security benefits in that they are discretionary, and Budgeting Loans and Crisis Loans have to be repaid. There is a limited budget for the discretionary Social Fund which restricts the overall amount that can be awarded in grants and loans in any financial year. There is a legal framework for the system and Social Fund decision makers have to follow legal rules called 'directions' and take account of guidance which helps them make decisions. For Community Care Grants and Crisis Loans they must consider all the individual circumstances of the people who apply and decide which applications can be met from the budget. Awards of Budgeting Loans are more 'fact-based', as explained below, rather than being wholly discretionary, but they must still be made from a fixed budget.

The £1,000 capital limit for Social Fund payments described here applies only to people aged 60 or over. For younger people, a capital limit of £500 applies.

Community Care Grants

These are available to people on Income Support or income-based Jobseeker's Allowance and to people who will be discharged from care within six weeks and are likely to receive these benefits on discharge. The grants do not have to be repaid. The amount of savings over £1,000 (£500 for people under 60) will be deducted from any grant awarded. For example, if you have £1,100 savings and you need an item costing £300 you would only receive a grant for £200. If you are not sure whether you will get help, you have nothing to lose by applying. It is important to include all the relevant information (see below on 'How to apply').

Grants are available for certain purposes including:

- help with moving out of institutional or residential care (eg for a bed, a cooker, fuel connection or removal costs);
- help to enable you to remain living at home (eg for minor house repairs, bedding and essential furniture, removal costs to more suitable accommodation);
- help with exceptional pressures on families (eg caused by disability, chronic sickness or a breakdown in a relationship); and
- help with certain travel expenses (eg for visiting someone who is ill or attending a relative's funeral).

For details of the other purposes for which grants can be paid, see social security guide SB 16.

Budgeting Loans

These are available to people who have been receiving Income Support or income-based Jobseeker's Allowance for at least 26 weeks. They enable people to spread the cost of one-off expenses over a longer period. The loans, which are interest-free, have to be repaid, and the amount of any savings over £1,000 (£500 for people under 60) will reduce the amount of the loan.

The applications for Budgeting Loans and Community Care Grants are separate. Therefore you should consider whether you might qualify for a grant before applying for a Budgeting Loan.

You may be able to get a Budgeting Loan for items such as furniture and household equipment, clothing and footwear, removal costs or home improvements or maintenance. In deciding whether you can be awarded a loan, the Social Fund decision maker will look at the time you have been on benefit, the people in your household and any loans you have already had from the Social Fund.

Crisis Loans

These interest-free loans are available to anyone (not just people on Income Support or income-based Jobseeker's Allowance) who needs something urgently in an emergency or as a result of a disaster (eg fire or flood). The Social Fund decision maker will take into account any family savings or income which is available to you. You may be able to get a loan provided that this is the only way of preventing serious damage or risk to your health or safety or that of a member of your family.

Repayment of loans

Budgeting or Crisis Loans will be awarded only if the officer thinks you will be able to repay them. Normally repayments will be deducted from your benefit over a period of 78 weeks. In special circumstances the repayment period may be extended further.

The repayment rates will be fixed after taking into account your income and your existing commitments. In the case of Crisis Loans, repayments will not normally begin until after the period of crisis is over.

How to apply

To apply for a Community Care Grant you will need form SF300 and for a Budgeting Loan you need application form SF 500 from your local social security office. If you need a Crisis Loan, ask at the office for an application form.

When applying for a Community Care Grant or Crisis Loan you should give as much information as possible about your circumstances and why you need help (eg health problems). If there is not enough room on the form, use a separate sheet.

A welfare rights agency or Citizens Advice Bureau may be able to help you with the application. You may also wish to include a letter of support from your GP or social worker.

If you are unhappy about a decision

Community Care Grants and loans from the Social Fund are discretionary payments. If you disagree with a decision, you cannot appeal to an appeal tribunal, but instead there is a special system of review. The first stage of review is at the local office, and you are given the chance to put your case personally to a Social Fund Reviewing Officer. If you are still dissatisfied, you can take your case to the Independent Review Service where it will be considered by a Social Fund Inspector, who is independent of your local social security office. A local advice agency may be able to help if you want to ask for a review.

See social security leaflet GL 18 or detailed guide SB 16 for more information about the Social Fund.

HOUSING BENEFIT AND COUNCIL TAX BENEFIT

Housing Benefit provides help with rent, with certain service charges and, in Northern Ireland, with general rates. People who live in Northern Ireland and require information about rate rebates should contact Age Concern Northern Ireland.

Council Tax Benefit is a social security benefit which provides help with paying the Council Tax. See also 'Help with the Council Tax' on pages 118–119, which gives information about other ways your Council Tax bill may be reduced which are not related to your income or savings.

You may get Housing Benefit or Council Tax Benefit if you have a low income and your savings are no more than £16,000. You must also be 'habitually resident' in the UK, and not excluded from claiming because of your immigration status. If you have a partner (that is, you are married or live with someone of the opposite sex as though you were married), the amount of benefit you get will be worked out on your combined savings and income. Housing Benefit and Council Tax Benefit are not taxable.

Who qualifies for Housing Benefit?

You may get Housing Benefit if you are responsible for paying rent and you fulfil the conditions outlined above. Benefit is available to council, housing association and private tenants and to people in the following circumstances:

Boarders and people living in hostels may get Housing Benefit for the accommodation part of their charges and may also get Income Support or income-based Jobseeker's Allowance (see page 54).

People living in a houseboat may get benefit for the mooring charges even if they own the houseboat.

People living in a caravan or mobile home may get help with the site charges even if they own the caravan or mobile home.

Joint tenants may receive Housing Benefit towards the part of the costs for which they are responsible.

People living with a landlord who is a close relative may claim Housing Benefit if they live separately in self-contained accommodation. However, they cannot claim benefit if they are part of the same household, or if it is not a 'commercial arrangement'. Get advice if you are unsure about your position.

Who qualifies for Council Tax Benefit?

There are two types of Council Tax Benefit – 'main Council Tax Benefit' and 'second adult rebate'. If you are responsible for paying the Council Tax, you may be able to receive main Council Tax Benefit provided that you fulfil the conditions outlined above. If you are jointly responsible for a bill with someone other than your partner, you can apply for help with your share of the tax.

The second adult rebate may be available to some people, regardless of their income and savings, who have one or more people with low incomes living with them. This is covered on page 74, while the rest of this section covers the main benefit scheme.

How to work out your benefit

Housing Benefit and Council Tax Benefit are worked out using similar calculations. The rules outlined below apply to both benefits unless stated otherwise. To work out how much benefit you will get, follow the steps listed, which are then explained.

1　Calculate the maximum weekly rent and Council Tax for which you can get benefit.
2　Deduct an amount for non-dependants living in your home.
3　Add up the value of your savings, but note that certain types of savings are ignored.
4　Add up your weekly income, but note that certain kinds of income are ignored.

5 Work out the amount the Government says you need to live on, called the 'applicable amount'.
6 Calculate your benefit according to the formula explained below.
7 For Housing Benefit, check that the benefit is above the minimum amount payable, which is 50p a week. There is no minimum payment for Council Tax Benefit.

1 Your rent and Council Tax

For Housing Benefit purposes, rent is the payment made to occupy your home. It also covers certain service charges – for example for furniture, cleaning communal areas, cleaning your rooms (if neither you nor your partner can do this), portering, entry phones, wardens and caretakers, rubbish removal. Also included in service charges is the cost of an emergency alarm system, but only if it has been installed in accommodation specially designed or adapted for older people or those with disabilities. Major changes are planned to the funding of services for residents of supported housing (including sheltered housing).

From April 2003 local authorities will receive a grant for funding support services. This means that the cost of support services, including those provided by wardens in sheltered housing, will no longer be funded through Housing Benefit. Instead the landlord will receive a grant from the local authority to pay for such services. At the time of writing full details of how this will work in practice are still being considered. Contact Age Concern England for more information at the address on page 157.

You cannot get benefit for water rates and sewerage charges. Homeowners cannot get Housing Benefit; however, they may get help with certain costs such as service charges and mortgage interest payments from Income Support or income-based Jobseeker's Allowance (see pages 51–53).

The maximum Housing Benefit you can get is 100 per cent of your rent including the service charges described above.

However, the level of rent on which benefit is calculated may be reduced, as explained below.

High rents

If the local authority considers that your rent is too high or your accommodation is larger than you need (taking into account your circumstances) or that the rent has increased unreasonably while you have been getting Housing Benefit, it may restrict the amount of Housing Benefit.

In addition, some private tenants may face further benefit restrictions if their rent is higher than the typical rent for similar accommodation in the area. These restrictions will not apply to people who were already receiving benefit before 2 January 1996 and have not moved since. Occasionally these rules might also apply to housing association tenants. Before taking up a tenancy, you can ask the local authority for a 'pre-tenancy determination', which will tell you how much of the rent would be eligible for Housing Benefit. Local authorities can make 'discretionary housing payments' if you need help with your rent or Council Tax. So if your benefit is restricted, you may want to apply for help under this scheme.

If you want to challenge a decision about your benefit or to ask the local authority to use its discretion, it is a good idea to get advice from a local agency. The rules on rent restrictions are complicated and are only covered briefly here. If you need more information, contact Age Concern or consult a book such as the *Welfare Benefits Handbook* (see page 155).

Council Tax

The maximum Council Tax Benefit you can get is 100 per cent of your bill. However, since 1 April 1998 benefit has been restricted for new claimants who live in properties in bands F, G and H. In this situation your benefit will only be calculated on the basis of the level of Council Tax for a band E property in your area. The restrictions will not apply if you were receiving Council Tax Benefit on 31 March 1998 as long as you remain in the same property and do not have a break in benefit entitlement of more than 12 weeks.

Council Tax Benefit is based on the amount you are asked to pay after any 'discounts' or 'reductions' (see pages 118–119) have been given. For example, if you live alone you will receive a 25 per cent discount on your bill, and your benefit will be worked out after this has been deducted.

● Note that the calculations in this section are all done on a weekly basis. So if you pay your Council Tax in ten monthly instalments, you will first have to work out how much this would be per week over the whole year.

Heating charges

Some people have a charge for heating included in their rent. You cannot get Housing Benefit for heating and other fuel charges. If, for example, you pay £45 a week rent and £5 of that is for heating, you will only get a maximum of £40 Housing Benefit, as the charge for fuel will be deducted.

If your weekly fuel charges are not stated as a separate amount, the council will deduct the amounts listed below:

Heating	£9.40
Hot water	£1.15
Cooking	£1.15
Lighting	£0.80
All fuel	£12.50

The amounts are lower if you occupy only one room.

2 Deductions for non-dependants living in your home

A deduction will normally be made from both your Housing Benefit and your Council Tax Benefit if you have someone else living with you who is not your partner or a dependent child nor a joint tenant or joint owner. This is because people such as grown-up sons and daughters (called 'non-dependants') are expected to contribute to housing costs. However, no deduction will be made if you or your partner is blind or receives Attendance Allowance or the care component of Disability Living Allowance. There are also some types of non-dependant who do not give rise to a deduction – for example, students or people in hospital for more than six weeks.

If the person living with you is aged 18 or over, works 16 hours a week or more, and has a gross income of at least £88 a week, the rates of deduction are as follows:

Gross income of non-dependant	Weekly deduction from rent	Weekly deduction from Council Tax
£88.00 to £130.99	£17.00	£2.30
£131.00 to £169.99	£23.35	£4.60
£170.00 to £224.99	£38.20	£4.60
£225.00 to £280.99	£43.50	£5.80
£281 or more	£47.75	£6.95

If the person who lives with you receives Income Support or income-based Jobseeker's Allowance (JSA), there will be no deduction from your Housing Benefit if they are under 25 and a £7.40 deduction if they are aged 25 or over. There will be a £7.40 deduction from your Housing Benefit for anyone else who is aged 18 or over and does not fall into any of the categories already mentioned.

For Council Tax Benefit there is no deduction for a non-dependant receiving Income Support or income-based JSA while for others aged 18 or over not covered above there will be a £2.30 deduction.

Only one deduction is made for a non-dependent couple living with you.

3 Your savings

Throughout this book the term 'savings' is used to cover savings, capital, investments and property.

If your savings are more than £16,000, you cannot get Housing Benefit or Council Tax Benefit. For a couple, savings are added together, but the limit is the same. If you are aged 60 or over you can have up to £6,000 in savings without it affecting your benefit. For a couple at least one partner must be aged 60 or over. For younger people the amount of savings that is not taken into account is £3,000.

If you have savings of between £6,000 (£3,000 for people under 60) and £16,000, an income of £1 a week for every £250 (or part of £250) over £6,000 (or £3,000) will be taken into account in working out your benefit. For example, a 70-year old with savings of £6,480 will be treated as having an income of £2 a week. Savings of £10,760 will be treated as £20 a week. This is called 'tariff income'. Savings of £6,000 (£3,000 if you are under 60) or less will not affect your benefit.

● **If you 'deprive' yourself of savings in order to get benefit or to increase the amount of benefit, you will be considered as still having those savings. Depriving yourself of savings might include giving money away to your family or buying expensive items in order to gain benefit. You should seek advice if you are refused benefit because of this.**

Savings and capital are normally valued at their current market or surrender value. If there are expenses involved in selling them, 10 per cent will be deducted. Most forms of savings and capital will be taken into account, including:

● cash;
● bank and building society accounts (including current accounts that do not pay interest);
● National Savings accounts and certificates (valued according to rules which the local authority will explain);
● premium bonds;
● stocks and shares;

- property; and
- a share of any savings you own jointly with other people – these will be divided equally by the number of joint owners to calculate your share.

Some types of savings and capital will be ignored, including:

- the value of your home if you own it and are living there;
- the surrender value of a life assurance policy (although if a policy is cashed in the money you receive will normally be counted);
- arrears of certain benefits such as Attendance Allowance, DLA or Income Support for 52 weeks from the date you receive them;
- your personal possessions, unless they have been bought in order to reduce your savings; and
- the £10,000 ex-gratia payment for Far Eastern Prisoners of War (see page 107).

Your money should not normally be counted as both 'income' and 'savings'. So if, for example, your pension is paid four-weekly into a bank account, this should not be assessed as part of your savings unless it is still unspent at the end of the four-week period.

4 Your income

Income includes earnings, State pensions and benefits, occupational or personal pensions and any other money you have coming in after tax and NI contributions have been paid. For a couple, the income of both partners is added together when calculating benefit.

However, some income may be fully or partly ignored when your benefit is calculated. Income that will be fully ignored includes:

- Income Support;
- Disability Living Allowance;
- Attendance Allowance;

- actual interest or income from savings or capital of £16,000 or less (only tariff income will be counted, as explained above). Interest is not counted as income but once it is paid into an account it will be counted as part of your savings;
- the special war widow's pension for 'pre-1973 widows', which is now £59.95 (in addition to the £10 of a War Widow's Pension outlined below); and
- payments made to you (for example by a relative or charity) for things not covered by benefit such as telephone costs, TV rental or holidays, as long as you actually use them for these purposes.

The following are examples of parts of weekly income that will also be ignored:

- £5 of your earnings if you work part-time and are single;
- £10 of your or your partner's earnings from part-time work;
- £20 of earnings if you work part-time and you are a carer receiving the carer premium or in certain circumstances when you or your partner is disabled (instead of the £5 or £10 listed above);
- £10 of a War Widow's Pension or War Disablement Pension (the local authority has the discretion to increase the amount from these pensions that is ignored when working out your benefit, but not all authorities operate such schemes);
- £20 of regular payments from a friend, relative or charity, unless these are fully ignored, as described above (but this £20 will not be ignored on top of £10 from a war pension because the total amount from these two types of income that can be ignored must not be more than £20);
- £4 of any payment from a subtenant living in your home;
- £13.40 of any payment from a subtenant which includes an amount for heating; and
- £20 income from a boarder plus half of the boarder's charge over £20.

To work out your benefit, decide what kinds of income will be ignored and add up the remainder (including tariff income for savings between £6,000 (£3,000 if you are under 60) and £16,000).

5 Your applicable amount

This is the weekly amount intended to meet your day-to-day living needs. If your income is higher than this, you may still get some help with rent and the Council Tax.

Your applicable amount for Housing Benefit and Council Tax Benefit is worked out in the same way as for Income Support except that there are no additions for the housing costs of homeowners. To work out your applicable amount, add up the personal allowance and any premiums that apply to you (see pages 45–49).

6 Calculating Housing Benefit and Council Tax Benefit

Once you have worked out your applicable amount, compare this figure with your income, including any tariff income from savings over £6,000 (£3,000 if you are aged under 60). If your income is the same as or less than your applicable amount, you will normally get all your rent and Council Tax paid (unless, for example, there are deductions for ineligible service charges, for other people living in your home or because your rent or Council Tax band is considered too high).

If your income is more than your applicable amount, the maximum benefit you can get is reduced. You first work out the difference between your income and your applicable amount. The maximum Housing Benefit payable is reduced by 65 per cent of this difference. The maximum Council Tax Benefit is reduced by 20 per cent of the difference.

Another way of explaining the calculation is to say that your maximum Housing Benefit is reduced by 65p for every pound that your income is more than your applicable amount. Your maximum Council Tax Benefit is reduced by 20p for every pound that your income is more than your applicable amount.

Example

Julie Walker is aged 64 and lives alone. Her income consists of
a State Pension (Basic and Additional Pension) of £84 a week
and the mobility component of Disability Living Allowance of
£39.30 a week. She has £2,000 savings and pays £40 a week
rent and £7 a week Council Tax (after the 25% discount
because she lives alone).

The maximum Housing Benefit she can get is £40 a week
(100% of her rent). The maximum Council Tax Benefit she can
get is £7 a week (100% of her Council Tax). There are no non-
dependant deductions because she lives alone.

Her savings will not affect her benefit and her Disability Living
Allowance is ignored. Her income is £84.

Julie's applicable amount is set out below

Personal allowance	£53.95
Premium for age 60+	£44.20
Total	£98.15

Her income is less than her applicable amount, so she will get
the maximum Housing Benefit of £40 a week for rent and the
maximum Council Tax Benefit of £7 a week. She will also
qualify for Income Support and should make a claim.

Example

Nimesh and Anila Khan are both aged 68 and live in a rented
house. They pay £58 a week rent which includes £8 heating.
Their Council Tax is £11 a week. They have a State Pension of
£120.70 a week, Nimesh's occupational pension of £43.10 a
week, and savings of £7,400.

The maximum Housing Benefit they can get is £50 (£58 minus
the heating charge of £8). The maximum Council Tax Benefit
they can get is £11. They have nobody else living with them so
there will be no non-dependant deductions.

Nimesh and Anila add up their income

State Pension	£120.70
Occupational pension	£43.10
Tariff income (for savings over £6,000)	£6.00
Total	£169.80

They calculate their applicable amount

Personal allowance	£84.65
Premium for age 60+	£65.15
Total	£149.80

Their income is more than their applicable amount, the difference being £20 (£169.80 – £149.80).

Their weekly benefit is worked out in the following way

Rent

100% of rent	£50.00
Less 65% of difference	
(65% of £20)	£13.00
Housing Benefit	£37.00

Council Tax

100% of tax	£11.00
Less 20% of difference	
(20% of £20)	£4.00
Council Tax Benefit	£7.00

Total benefit is

Housing Benefit	£37.00
Council Tax Benefit	£7.00

Nimesh and Anila will have to pay £13 a week for rent plus the £8 heating charge and £4 towards the Council Tax.

If their son, who is 35, works 30 hours a week and earns £165 a week, comes to live with them their Housing Benefit will be reduced by £23.35 and their Council Tax Benefit by £4.60 a

week. They would therefore get £13.65 a week Housing
Benefit and £2.40 a week Council Tax Benefit.

Second adult rebate

If you are solely liable to pay the Council Tax, you might get a
second adult rebate if one or more people with a low income
live with you, regardless of the level of your savings and
income. This will usually apply only to people who do not have
a partner. You may get a 25 per cent rebate if you are
responsible for the Council Tax and you have one or more
people receiving Income Support or income-based Jobseeker's
Allowance (JSA) living with you. A 15 per cent rebate is given if
the person or people living with you have a joint gross income
of less than £131; there is a 7.5 per cent rebate if their income
is £131 or more, up to £169.99. In assessing the income of
people living with you, no account is taken of Attendance
Allowance, Disability Living Allowance or the income of
anyone receiving Income Support or income-based JSA.

Example

Janice Grant is a widow who owns her own home. Her son is
living with her and receives income-based JSA. Her Council Tax
bill for the year is £600. She is not entitled to the main Council
Tax Benefit because she has £18,000 savings. However, she
applies for a rebate and receives the second adult rebate of
25 per cent (£150) because her son receives income-based JSA.

Some people will be entitled to the main Council Tax Benefit
and the second adult rebate. In this case the local authority will
award you whichever benefit will give you the greater amount.

Only brief details have been given here as this system can be
complicated, so contact your local authority or advice agency if
you need further information.

Benefit for people in different circumstances

Absence from home

If you go into hospital on a temporary basis, you can continue to get Housing Benefit and Council Tax Benefit for up to 52 weeks (provided that you intend to return home). However, the amount you receive may be reduced after six weeks. If you are temporarily away from home for other reasons, benefit will be paid for up to 13 weeks or up to 52 weeks depending on the reason for your absence. Contact the local authority or local advice agency if you need more information about this. You cannot get benefit if you sub-let your home while you are away.

Benefit for two homes

You can normally only get Housing Benefit for one home. However, there are some circumstances in which payments may be made for two homes. For example, you may qualify for benefit on two homes for up to four weeks if you have moved to a new home and it is reasonable that you could not avoid liability to make payments for both homes. Another example is where your move to a new home has been delayed because it was being adapted to meet disability needs. Entitlement to Housing Benefit for two homes is not automatic, so ask your local authority whether you qualify.

Council Tax Benefit is payable only for the home in which you normally live. It is not payable for second homes.

Discretionary housing payments

You can apply to the local authority for an extra payment towards your rent and Council Tax if you are having difficulty meeting your bills. Your local authority will tell you how to make a claim and you will be able to give reasons why you need additional support.

How to claim

If you are claiming Income Support or income-based Jobseeker's Allowance, you will also be given claim forms for Housing Benefit and Council Tax Benefit. After any entitlement to Income Support or income-based JSA has been worked out, the local authority will be notified so that it can calculate your Housing Benefit and Council Tax Benefit. The local authority may send you a further form to complete.

If you are not claiming Income Support or income-based JSA, you claim Housing Benefit and Council Tax Benefit directly from your local authority.

If you are a couple, only one of you should claim for benefit – it does not matter if the bill is sent in joint names or just to one of you. Your benefit will be calculated on the basis of your combined income and savings.

Before the local authority can work out how much to pay, it may require evidence such as details of your income, savings and the amount of rent you pay. Benefit is normally awarded for a fixed period of up to 60 weeks, and you will receive another claim form to make a fresh claim at the end of this period.

The local authority can backdate your claim for benefit for up to 52 weeks if you can show that you had a good reason for claiming late. You should let the local authority know about any changes in your circumstances that might affect your benefit. Otherwise you may lose benefit or receive too much which you may have to pay back.

It has been announced that from April 2003 there will be changes to the rules regarding claims and changes of circumstances, as explained on page 57.

Delays and administrative problems

The local authority should let you know within 14 days of your claim whether you qualify for help as long as you have provided any information and evidence needed. However, this sometimes takes much longer and in some areas of the country there are problems with the administration of benefit. If you are suffering hardship because the local authority has not yet worked out your claim for benefit or you are having problems with your benefit, contact your nearest Citizens Advice Bureau or advice centre for help.

How it is paid

For council tenants, Housing Benefit is usually paid by reducing the rent. If you are a private or housing association tenant, your Housing Benefit may be paid to you by cheque or into a bank account or direct to your landlord.

Most people will pay the Council Tax direct to their local authority, so when you claim benefit your bill will be reduced accordingly. Where this is not possible because, for example, you have already paid the whole bill, the local authority may send you a refund or credit your account.

Overpayment

If you are paid too much benefit, this is known as an overpayment and in most circumstances the council can ask you to repay this money. However, an overpayment cannot normally be recovered if it was caused by an 'official error' and you could not reasonably be expected to have known you were being overpaid at the time. Even if the local authority can recover the benefit, it does have some discretion about whether to do so. It is a good idea to seek further advice if you are being asked to repay benefit.

If you disagree with a decision

If you disagree with a decision about your Housing Benefit or Council Tax Benefit, you can ask for the decision to be revised or appeal to an independent tribunal (see pages 32–35). Before July 2001 there was a different review system but the way to challenge a decision is now in line with that for most other social security benefits.

Benefits for People with Disabilities and Their Carers

This part of Your Rights *describes the main benefits available to people with disabilities and those who look after them.*

Disability Living Allowance and Attendance Allowance are intended to help with the extra costs associated with disability while other benefits such as Incapacity Benefit and Invalid Care Allowance are paid to people who are unable to work or can work only to a limited extent because of their disability or because they are a carer.

ATTENDANCE ALLOWANCE AND DISABILITY LIVING ALLOWANCE

Attendance Allowance and Disability Living Allowance (DLA) are intended to provide help towards the extra costs arising from illness or disability. You can claim either Attendance Allowance or DLA. Which one you claim depends on your age.

To qualify for DLA you must need help with personal care or need supervision and/or have difficulty getting around, and you must claim before your 65th birthday. If you are 65 or over, you should claim Attendance Allowance instead.

This section covers first the conditions for Attendance Allowance and then the conditions for Disability Living Allowance; the third part gives information that applies to both allowances.

Attendance Allowance

This is a benefit for people aged 65 or over who need help with personal care, or need supervision, or need someone to watch over them because of physical or mental illness or disability. It does not depend on National Insurance (NI) contributions, is not affected by savings or income, and will not normally affect or be affected by other benefits or pensions received. Attendance Allowance is not taxable.

There are two weekly rates:

Higher rate	£56.25
Lower rate	£37.65

Who qualifies for Attendance Allowance?

To qualify for Attendance Allowance you must fulfil all the following conditions:

- You are aged 65 or older.
- You meet the day and/or night conditions described below.
- You must also normally have satisfied the disability conditions for at least six months, but there are 'special rules' for people who are terminally ill, as explained on page 89.
- You are normally resident in the UK when you make your claim, and (unless you are applying under the special rules for terminally ill people) have been here for at least 26 weeks of the last 12 months.

You will receive the lower rate if you fulfil either the day or the night conditions. You will get the higher rate if you fulfil both day and night conditions.

You can receive the allowance if you live alone or with other people and regardless of whether or not you receive any help from someone else – what matters is that you need help with personal care, supervision or watching over, not whether you are actually getting help. You do not have to spend the allowance on paying for care: it is up to you how you use it. However, your local authority may take it into account when assessing whether, and how much, you need to pay for any care services you have.

Day conditions

You can get the allowance if you are so disabled that you require frequent help throughout the day with your normal 'bodily functions' such as eating, getting in or out of bed, going to the toilet or washing. 'Seeing' and 'hearing' are considered bodily functions. For example, if you are visually impaired and need guidance when walking or someone to read your mail, or if you are deaf and need help with communicating, this could help you satisfy the requirement for needing 'frequent help'. You can also get the allowance if you need continual supervision throughout the day to avoid putting yourself or others in substantial danger.

Night conditions

You can also get the allowance if you are so disabled that you require prolonged (periods of at least 20 minutes) or repeated (at least twice nightly) attention during the night to help you with your bodily functions – for example, going to the toilet and getting in and out of bed. You can also get the allowance if another person needs to be awake for a prolonged period or at frequent intervals throughout the night in order to watch over you to avoid putting yourself or others in substantial danger.

The next section covers the qualifying conditions for Disability Living Allowance. You should turn to pages 86–90 for information that covers both allowances such as how to make a claim and what happens if you are away from home.

Disability Living Allowance

This benefit replaced Attendance Allowance and Mobility Allowance for people who become ill or disabled and make a claim before the age of 65. It is for disabled people who:

- need help with personal care, or need supervision, or need someone to watch over them; or
- are unable to walk, have great difficulty walking, or need someone with them when walking outdoors; or
- need help with both of these.

Disability Living Allowance (DLA) does not depend on NI contributions, is not affected by savings or income, and will not normally affect other benefits or pensions received. DLA is not taxable.

There are two parts to DLA: the 'care component', which is paid at one of three rates, and the 'mobility component', which has two different levels. The weekly rates are:

DLA care component		DLA mobility component	
Highest rate	£56.25	Higher rate	£39.30
Middle rate	£37.65	Lower rate	£14.90
Lowest rate	£14.90		

Who qualifies for DLA?

To qualify for DLA you must fulfil the following conditions:

- You meet one or more of the care or mobility conditions described below.
- You are aged under 65.
- You must also normally have satisfied the disability conditions for at least three months, and be expected to satisfy them for at least the next six months, but there are 'special rules' for people who are terminally ill, as explained on page 89.
- You are normally resident in the UK when you make your claim, and (unless you are applying under the special rules for terminally ill people) have been here for at least 26 weeks of the last 12 months.

Although you must have become disabled, and made a claim, before the age of 65, once you are awarded the allowance it will continue, without an age limit, as long as you satisfy either the care or the mobility conditions. Your entitlement may be reviewed after you reach 65, but after that age you cannot be awarded either of the mobility component rates nor the lower rate of the care component.

The care component

The care component of DLA is for people who need help with personal care, supervision or watching over because of physical or mental illness or disability. It does not matter if you live alone or with other people, or whether or not you receive any help from someone else – what matters is that you need help with personal care, supervision or watching over, not whether you are actually getting help. You do not have to spend the allowance on paying for care: it is up to you how you use it. However, your local authority may take it into account when assessing whether, and how much, you need to pay for any care services you have.

You will receive £14.90 if you fulfil the lower-rate conditions but not the day or night conditions described below. You will receive the middle level if you fulfil either the day or the night conditions while the highest level is for those who fulfil both day and night conditions. You will see that the day and night conditions are the same as those for Attendance Allowance.

Lower-rate conditions

You will fulfil this condition if you need help with 'bodily functions' for a significant portion of the day, either at one single period or a number of times. For example, you might need some help to get up in the morning and go to bed in the evening but manage alone for the rest of the day. You will also fulfil this condition if you could not prepare a main cooked meal for yourself even if you had the ingredients.

Day conditions

You will fulfil this condition if you are so disabled that you require frequent help throughout the day with your normal bodily functions such as eating, getting in or out of bed, going to the toilet or washing. 'Seeing' and 'hearing' are considered bodily functions. For example, if you are visually impaired and need guidance when walking or someone to read your mail, or you are deaf and need help with communicating, this could help you satisfy the requirement for needing 'frequent help'. You can also get the allowance if you need continual supervision throughout the day to avoid putting yourself or others in substantial danger.

Night conditions

You will fulfil this condition if you are so disabled that you require prolonged (periods of at least 20 minutes) or repeated (at least twice nightly) attention during the night to help you with your bodily functions – for example, going to the toilet and getting in and out of bed. You can also get the allowance if another person needs to be awake for a prolonged period or at frequent intervals throughout the night in order to watch over you to avoid putting yourself or others in substantial danger.

The mobility component

Although the mobility component is given to people who need help getting around, you can spend it how you choose. Remember that it is not available to people who become disabled after the age of 65.

You can receive the higher level if you are unable to walk or have great difficulty in walking because of a physical disability. The higher level is also available to people who are both blind and deaf and need someone with them when outdoors, to all people who have lost both legs at or above the ankle, and to certain severely mentally disabled people who have severe behavioural problems. If you can walk but need someone with you for guidance or supervision, you may be awarded the lower level.

Using a car

If you own a car and get the higher mobility component of DLA, you may not have to pay road tax. If someone drives a car for you, they can also apply for exemption from road tax. You will get details about this and about getting a car through the Motability Scheme when you first get the allowance.

You can also apply to the local authority for a blue badge (formerly an orange badge) which allows parking with some limitations but without charge at meters or where waiting is restricted. Some local authorities make a small charge for issuing the badge.

Examples of people who may receive DLA

Ellen Johnson is 62 and cannot walk very far owing to severe osteo-arthritis in her hips and hands. Although she can manage to care for herself, she finds cooking very difficult because she cannot do tasks such as cutting, lifting and pouring. She applied for DLA and was awarded the higher level of the mobility component and the lowest level of the care component.

Albert Brown is 64 and suffers from dementia. During the day his wife or another relative stays with him all the time because he is very forgetful and sometimes wanders off or turns on the gas without lighting it. He normally sleeps all through the night. His wife applied for DLA on his behalf and he was awarded the middle level of the care component (because he needs guidance and supervision during the day) and the lower level of the mobility component because he needs guidance when outdoors.

Sarah Bloom is 68 and had a severe stroke six months ago which left her unable to walk and needing a lot of help, for example with washing, dressing and eating. Because she is 68 she is too old to claim DLA. She cannot get any help with her mobility needs but she can apply for Attendance Allowance because she needs personal care.

Remember that these are just examples and your situation is probably different. Whether you qualify for DLA, and if so at what level, will depend on your particular circumstances.

Rules covering both Attendance Allowance and Disability Living Allowance

If you are away from home

If you are receiving NHS treatment in a hospital, you cannot start to receive Attendance Allowance or DLA (although you can make a claim and, if you fulfil the conditions, the allowance can be paid when you go home). However, you may receive either of these allowances if you are a private patient paying for the cost of hospital services.

If you are already receiving Attendance Allowance or DLA and you go into hospital, you will be able to continue to receive the allowance for up to four weeks. However, the allowance will stop sooner if your admission is within 28 days of a previous stay in hospital.

Before July 1996, a stay in hospital did not normally affect the mobility component of DLA. Some people in hospital for 12 months or more in July 1996 received transitional protection and can continue to get an amount equivalent to the lower rate of the mobility component.

For information about Attendance Allowance and DLA for people in care homes, see pages 129–130. In general, a holiday abroad does not affect Attendance Allowance or DLA, nor do periods abroad for medical treatment. You should let your social security office know when you intend to go abroad so that payment of the allowance while you are abroad can be considered.

How to claim

The claim forms for Attendance Allowance and DLA are quite long; the intention is that people can describe how their disability affects them. This means that a medical examination will not normally be necessary. Do not be put off by the length of the form. If you have difficulties filling it in, a friend or relative can fill in the form for you. A local advice agency may be able to help, or you can telephone the Benefits Enquiry Line for advice on Freephone 0800 88 22 00. If it is difficult for you to get out, your local social security office may be able to arrange for a visiting officer to call to help you with the form.

There are two sections of the form: Section 1 deals with information about yourself and Section 2 asks about how your disability or illness affects you.

If you have difficulty with the second section or would rather have a medical examination, you can ask for a doctor to visit. When filling in the second section, remember that it does not matter if you actually receive any help or not. Be sure to say what activities are difficult or impossible for you to do. For example, you may have to get dressed on your own because there is no one to help you but do explain if it takes a long time or if it is difficult. If you feel that having answered the questions you have not given a good picture of how your disability affects you, add any extra information you think would be helpful. If you have any problems with filling in the form, do ask for help. There is also a space on the form for your doctor or someone else who knows about your circumstances to complete.

If your claim cannot be decided from the information in the form, the DWP may ask for further information from someone such as your doctor or district nurse, or it may arrange a medical examination. If an appointment is made for a doctor to visit, you may want a friend or relative to be there at that time. This will be particularly important if you have difficulty making yourself understood. The doctor, who will not be your own doctor but one appointed by the DWP, will probably examine you and ask further questions. It may be useful to make a note beforehand of the things you need to tell the doctor about when you need help or the difficulties you experience.

You can get the claim pack for Attendance Allowance or DLA from the local social security office, or by telephoning the Benefit Enquiry Line on 0800 88 22 00 or by sending off the tear-off slip on leaflet DS 702 (Attendance Allowance) or DS 704 (DLA). You should return the form in the envelope provided within six weeks or you may lose some benefit.

When to claim

Although you normally need to fulfil the qualifying conditions for three months before you can start getting DLA and six months for Attendance Allowance, if you have only recently become disabled you should still apply as it may take some weeks to deal with your claim. If you are receiving a lower level of one of the allowances but your condition has deteriorated so you might now qualify for a higher level, you can ask for your case to be reconsidered. You will need to satisfy the care or mobility conditions for the higher level for three months (DLA) or six months (Attendance Allowance) before it can be paid. You should be aware that if you ask for your case to be looked at again, there is a possibility that instead of awarding a higher level your benefit might be stopped or reduced. You may want to seek help from a local advice agency to discuss your position and to ensure that you include all the relevant information if you ask for your benefit to be reconsidered.

Effect on other benefits

Sometimes if you become entitled to Attendance Allowance or DLA this will also enable you to start receiving other benefits such as Income Support (Minimum Income Guarantee) or Housing Benefit because these benefits can be higher if you are receiving a disability benefit. To ensure any benefit entitlement is backdated you need to claim these other benefits at the same time as you claim Attendance Allowance or DLA. If you are not sure of your position get help from a local advice agency.

Terminal illness

People who are terminally ill can claim DLA or Attendance Allowance without the three-month or six-month waiting period. They will be considered to be terminally ill if they have a progressive illness that is likely to limit their life expectancy to six months or less.

To claim ask your doctor for a DS 1500 report, which gives details of your condition. Send this in the envelope provided after completing Section 1 of the Attendance Allowance or DLA form, ensuring that you have ticked the special rules box on page 2. You do not need to complete the section which covers 'Help with personal care': if you are assessed as being terminally ill, you will automatically receive the higher rate of Attendance Allowance or the highest level of the care component of DLA. However, if you are under the age of 65 and you want to claim the mobility component of DLA, you will need to fill in the section on 'Help with getting around' and include this with your claim. Claims should be handled within 10–14 days and a medical examination will not normally be necessary.

An application can be made by another person on behalf of someone who is terminally ill with or without their knowledge, so it is possible for people to receive an allowance under the special rules without knowing their prognosis.

How it is paid

Attendance Allowance or DLA may be awarded indefinitely or for a set period, in which case it will be reviewed at the end of this time. If your allowance is awarded for a fixed period you should be sent a renewal claim before the end of that period. There is a system of periodic review for DLA which means that you may be sent a questionnaire or receive a visit to check if your needs are still the same.

Attendance Allowance is either paid weekly and collected at the Post Office or paid four-weekly in arrears directly into a bank or building society account. If you are receiving another benefit or pension, they will normally be paid together. DLA is normally paid four-weekly unless you were getting Attendance Allowance by weekly order book before April 1992. However, people claiming under the special rules because they are terminally ill can get weekly payments.

If you disagree with a decision

If you disagree with a decision about your allowance, you can ask for the decision to be revised or make an appeal. You will be sent details about how to do this when you receive the decision. It is important to challenge a decision or get advice as quickly as possible because there are time limits for doing so which generally mean that you must take action within one month. See pages 32–35 for more information or look at the *Disability Rights Handbook* which has more detailed information (see page 155).

For Attendance Allowance see social security leaflet DS 702 and claim pack DS 2. For DLA see social security leaflet DS 704 and claim pack DLA 1. See also Age Concern Factsheet 34 *Attendance Allowance and Disability Living Allowance.*

INVALID CARE ALLOWANCE

This is a benefit for people who are unable to work full-time because they are caring for a severely disabled person for at least 35 hours a week. The benefit is not dependent on having paid NI contributions. Invalid Care Allowance (ICA) is taxable.

Do note that in some situations the person you care for could lose money if you start to receive ICA. This will apply to a disabled person who receives the severe disability premium as part of their Income Support, Housing Benefit or Council Tax Benefit. See pages 47–48 for more information about the severe disability premium.

The weekly rates of ICA are:

Carer   £42.45

Adult dependant   £25.35

The person being cared for must be receiving one of the allowances referred to below, such as Attendance Allowance. They do not have to be a relative and may live separately or with the carer.

Currently, ICA stops when caring ceases. The rules are expected to change, however, to allow it to be paid for up to eight weeks after the death of the person being cared for. At the time of writing, legislation is being considered by Parliament; if agreed to, this rule change is likely to start at the end of October 2002. The Government also intends to change the name of ICA to 'Carer's Allowance' in the future, possibly in April 2003.

Who qualifies?

To qualify you must spend at least 35 hours a week looking after someone who is receiving Attendance Allowance (higher or lower rate), the care component of Disability Living Allowance (middle or highest level), or Constant Attendance Allowance of £46 or more paid with an industrial, war or service pension.

At the time of writing, you must have started caring and have become entitled to ICA before the age of 65, although once you receive ICA it can continue to be paid after the age of 65. However, new legislation is being considered which would change the rules and would allow claims from people over 65. If this is agreed by Parliament, it is expected that this change will come into effect on 28 October 2002.

A claim can be backdated for up to three months. It is important to claim ICA even if the person you care for is still waiting to hear if they qualify for Attendance Allowance or DLA. You must also be resident in the UK and have lived here for at least 26 weeks out of the past 12 months.

You cannot get ICA if you earn more than £75 a week net. The extra £25.35 which can be claimed for a dependent adult will not be paid if that person earns more than £25.35 a week, including any occupational or personal pension. It also may not be paid if they are receiving a State pension or certain other benefits. When calculating the net earnings of the carer or their partner, certain work expenses are deducted.

Overlap with the State Pension and other benefits

If you are already getting £42.45 a week or more from certain other social security benefits or pensions, you may not be able to get ICA as well. This is because ICA 'overlaps' with some benefits including Incapacity Benefit, Retirement Pension and Widow's Pension. If you have a spouse or partner who is claiming an addition to their benefit for you, that addition will be reduced by the amount of ICA received.

However, if you have a low income it may still be worth claiming ICA even though it may not be paid in addition to your present benefit or pension. Although ICA is counted as income if you claim Income Support (Minimum Income Guarantee), Housing Benefit or Council Tax Benefit, people entitled to ICA may be able to get higher rates of these benefits, owing to the 'carer premium', as explained on page 48.

Example

Olive Zhukova is 62 and looks after her mother who gets Attendance Allowance. Olive has no savings and has a total income of £100.50 (State Pension of £75.50 and an occupational pension of £25 a week). She is not entitled to Income Support because her income is more than £98.15 – the basic Income Support level for someone over 60.

She applies for ICA but, although she satisfies the conditions, it cannot be paid because her State Pension is more than £42.45 – the level of ICA. However, because she is entitled to ICA her Income Support rate is now £122.95 – the basic rate of £98.15 plus the carer premium of £24.80. She is now entitled to £22.45 in Income Support to bring her pensions of £100.50 up to the Income Support rate.

If you are in this situation you should claim Income Support at the same time as you claim ICA; otherwise you may not get the benefit fully backdated.

Protecting your pension

If you are entitled to ICA, NI contributions will be automatically credited to protect your right to a future Retirement Pension unless you have retained the right to pay the married woman's reduced-rate contributions. If you receive another benefit instead and are not working regularly because you are caring for someone, you may get Home Responsibilities Protection (see pages 10–12).

ICA after pension age

If you are receiving ICA when you reach pension age (60 for women, 65 for men), it will be adjusted to take account of any Retirement Pension you draw. If your pension is £42.45 or more, the allowance will stop. If your pension is less than £42.45, the allowance will be reduced by the amount of pension received. If you are not entitled to a pension or do not claim one, ICA may continue.

At the time of writing, If you are still receiving ICA at the age of 65, it can continue to be paid even if you are no longer caring for a disabled person. However, once the rules change to allow people over 65 to claim ICA (see page 92), then it is expected that this rule will also change. If you become 65 after the time of this rule change, you will not be able to continue to receive ICA if you are no longer caring; carers who are already 65 will not be affected however.

If you are already over 65, you may be able to claim ICA when the age limit is changed. However, as explained above, ICA and the Retirement Pension 'overlap' – so if your pension is more than £42.45 you may not be better off from claiming unless you are entitled to the carer premium with a benefit such as Income Support.

How to claim ICA

To make a claim you will need claim pack DS 700. You can get this pack from your local social security office or by ringing the Benefit Enquiry Line on Freephone 0800 88 22 00. Under new rules that are being phased in you may need to attend an interview with a personal adviser as a condition of receiving benefit. The aim is to look at work options as well as providing information about other help available.

See social security claim pack DS 700 or information leaflet SD 4 *Caring for Someone?* Carers UK produces information for carers – see page 152 for the address.

STATUTORY SICK PAY

If you are an employee earning at least £75 a week and you are under 65, you will probably be entitled to Statutory Sick Pay (SSP) if you are off sick for at least four days in a row. This can continue for up to 28 weeks and it will be paid by your employer. The weekly rate is £63.25. You may also get sick pay from your employer's own scheme depending on the terms and conditions. SSP is taxable. Contact your employer for details.

If you are unable to work because of sickness but not entitled to SSP, for example because you are self-employed or unemployed, you may be entitled to Incapacity Benefit, as explained overleaf.

INCAPACITY BENEFIT

This is a benefit for people who are unable to work owing to illness or disability. It was introduced on 13 April 1995 and replaced Sickness Benefit and Invalidity Benefit. It is based on NI contributions (except for some people disabled early in life). It is not generally means-tested but for claims on or after 6 April 2001 a personal or occupational pension of more than £85 a week may reduce benefit, as explained below.

This section mainly covers the current rules for Incapacity Benefit. However, if you were transferred from Invalidity Benefit to Incapacity Benefit in April 1995, you may be covered by transitional rules, as explained on page 100.

There are three levels of Incapacity Benefit. If you are an employee, you will probably be paid Statutory Sick Pay (SSP) by your employer for the first 28 weeks that you are unable to work (see above). However, if you are not entitled to SSP, for example because you are self-employed or unemployed, you may be able to get the short-term lower rate of Incapacity Benefit for up to 28 weeks. The short-term higher rate of Incapacity Benefit is paid from 29 weeks to 52 weeks of incapacity while the long-term rate is paid after 52 weeks. (People who are terminally ill or who receive the highest rate of the care component of Disability Living Allowance (DLA) will receive the long-term rate from 29 weeks.) The long-term rate can continue up to pension age as long as you remain unable to work. The short-term higher rate and the long-term rate are taxable, but the short-term lower rate is not.

The weekly rates of Incapacity Benefit are:

Short-term lower rate (under pension age)	£53.50
Short-term higher rate (under pension age)	£63.25
Long-term rate	£70.95

If you become unable to work before the age of 45, you will receive an age addition which will be paid when you start to receive the long-term rate of Incapacity Benefit. There are two rates, depending on the age at which you become unable to work:

| Under 35 | £14.90 |
| 35–44 | £7.45 |

Who qualifies?

To qualify for Incapacity Benefit you must be assessed as incapable of work and be under pension age (60 for women, 65 for men) when your period of incapacity began.

You must normally also satisfy certain NI contribution conditions; however, there are exceptions to this for certain people disabled before the age of 25.

The incapacity test

For the first 28 weeks of incapacity you will normally only need to provide a medical certificate from your doctor stating that you are unable to do your normal job, if you have one.

After 28 weeks, or from the start of incapacity if you have not worked for 8 out of the 21 weeks prior to your claim, most people will have to undertake a 'personal capability assessment' (previously called the 'all work' test). This will involve a questionnaire and, in some cases, a medical examination, to decide whether you are incapable of any work – not just your normal job. However, you will not be subject to the incapacity test if you are terminally ill, receive the highest care component of DLA, are registered blind, have certain severe medical conditions, or in some circumstances when you are entitled to industrial disablement benefit or a war pension.

Increases for a husband or wife

You may be entitled to an increase for an adult dependant if your husband or wife is aged 60 or over (unless you are covered by the transitional rules for people previously receiving Invalidity Benefit). If you are receiving the long-term rate of Incapacity Benefit, the increase for a dependent is £42.45 a week. If you are receiving either of the short-term rates, and you are under pension age, the increase is £33.10.

However, these increases 'overlap' with any State Pension or certain other State benefits that your husband or wife is receiving. So if, for example, your wife had a State Pension of £50 a week, you would not be entitled to an increase for her; if her pension was £20 a week, the amount you could receive would be reduced by £20.

If your husband or wife has earnings of more than £53.95 a week (if you are getting the long-term rate) or £33.10 a week (for the short-term rate), then you cannot receive an adult dependency increase – in this context any occupational or personal pension your spouse receives will be counted as earnings.

Work and Incapacity Benefit

From April 2002 the 'therapeutic work' rules have been replaced by 'permitted work' rules. Under these new rules you are able to work for up to 16 hours a week, on average, and earn up to £66 a week for 26 weeks. In some cases this can be extended by a further 26 weeks if your adviser at the Jobcentre Plus office agrees that this would help you towards working 16 hours a week or more. After the 26 or 52 weeks you can only work and earn up to £20 a week unless you are in certain types of 'supported permitted work', such as work in a sheltered workshop, when you will be able to continue to earn up to £66 a week. You must tell the social security office that you are working. If you were already doing therapeutic work on 7 April 2002, before the changes, you may be able to carry on doing this until April 2003. For more information contact your social security office.

Occupational and personal pensions

If you make a claim for Incapacity Benefit on or after 6 April 2001 and you have an occupational and/or personal pension of more than £85 a week, this will reduce your benefit. For every £1 of pension more than £85, you will lose 50 pence of benefit.

Anyone receiving Incapacity Benefit before 6 April 2001 will not be affected, nor will new claimants in receipt of the highest rate of the care component of Disability Living Allowance.

When you reach pension age

The long-term rate of Incapacity Benefit cannot be paid after pension age. So once you reach pension age (60 for women, 65 for men), you should draw the State Pension. It will be worked out as explained in the section starting on page 2, although if you were receiving an age addition with your Incapacity Benefit this can be paid with your Retirement Pension as an invalidity addition (after the deduction of any Additional Pension and contracted decuctions).

If you become incapable of work before pension age and are receiving short-term Incapacity Benefit, this can continue until you have been unable to work for up to a year. For people over pension age the short-term lower rate of Incapacity Benefit is £68.05 a week and the higher rate is £70.95, although you may get less if you do not have enough contributions for a full Basic Pension. You may also receive Additional and Graduated Pension. There is an adult dependency increase of £40.80 which you may receive if your husband or wife is aged 60 or over – depending on any earnings, pensions or other benefits they receive.

How to claim

If you have been receiving Statutory Sick Pay (SSP), your employer will give you a claim form. If you have not been receiving SSP, contact your local Jobcentre Plus office.

Under rules that are being gradually introduced nationally, people claiming Incapacity Benefit (and other benefits for people of working age) will normally be required to attend a work-focussed interview as a condition of benefit. The aim is to look at work options as well as to provide information about what practical and financial help is available.

If you disagree with a decision

If you disagree with a decision about your benefit, you can ask for the decision to be revised or you can make an appeal, as explained on pages 32–35.

If you were receiving Invalidity Benefit on 12 April 1995

If you were transferred from Invalidity Benefit to Incapacity Benefit in April 1995 and have continued to receive Incapacity Benefit since then (without a break of more than eight weeks, or longer if covered by certain linking rules), you will be covered by the transitional rules. These rules were introduced to provide some protection against changes which could reduce the amount of benefit people received. If you are covered by the transitional rules, your Incapacity Benefit will not be taxable.

If you are covered by transitional rules, the basic rate of Incapacity Benefit is £70.95 (ie the same as the long-term rate for new claimants). The increase for a dependent husband or wife is also the same (£42.25) and this will be reduced by their pensions, benefits or earnings in the same way. However, if you were receiving an increase for a dependent husband or wife with your Invalidity Benefit, this can continue to be paid if your spouse is under 60. If you make a claim for the dependant's increase now, or there is a break of a certain length in entitlement, the rules described on pages 97–98 will apply, which means that your husband or wife must be aged 60 or over.

You may receive Invalidity Allowance if you were previously getting it with your Invalidity Benefit. The rates, which depend on the age at which you became unable to work, are:

Under 40	£14.90
40–49	£9.50
Men 50–59, women 50–54	£4.75

You may also receive an Additional Rate based on any entitlement to Additional Pension you built up between 1978 and 1991. However, the level of Additional Rate is frozen at the amount you were receiving with your Invalidity Benefit before April 1995 and will not be increased in future years. It also 'overlaps' with Invalidity Allowance, so your Additional Rate will reduce any Invalidity Allowance you are entitled to. In other respects the Incapacity Benefit rules are generally the same as for new claimants and are described on page 98, although some people who have been incapable of work since before 13 April 1995 are exempt from the personal capability assessment.

SEVERE DISABLEMENT ALLOWANCE

Severe Disablement Allowance (SDA) was abolished for new claimants on 6 April 2001. However, you can still receive it if you were entitled to the benefit on or before 5 April 2001 and have been receiving it continuously since then (although short breaks may be covered by certain linking rules). If you are already in receipt of SDA it can be paid as long as you continue to satisfy the entitlement conditions. It is a benefit for people who are incapable of working but who do not have enough contributions to get Incapacity Benefit.

If you are under pension age and become unable to work due to ill health, you may be able to claim Incapacity Benefit if you fulfil the contribution conditions or otherwise may be entitled to help through income-related benefits.

SDA is not based on NI contributions and is not taxable. The basic weekly rates are:

Claimant	£42.85
Adult dependant	£25.45

There are also additions for people who became unable to work before the age of 60; these are added to the basic rate of £42.85. The weekly rates are:

Under 40	£14.90
40–49	£9.50
50–59	£4.75

SDA is not means-tested but is taken into account if you apply for income-related benefits such as Income Support. Contact a local advice agency or write to Age Concern at the address on page 157 if you need more information about SDA.

If you applied on or after 13 April 1995, you will only have received the adult dependency increase for your husband or wife if they are aged 60 or over. If they have earnings over

£53.95 or receive a State pension or benefit of £25.45 or over, you may not be able to get this increase. If you have been receiving the increase since before 13 April 1995 it can continue, even if your husband or wife is under 60.

SDA can continue to be paid after you reach pension age but it 'overlaps' with certain other benefits and so is not paid in addition to certain other State benefits or pensions. You cannot receive both the full amount of SDA and a Retirement Pension. If you do not qualify for a Retirement Pension or it is less than SDA, you can continue to receive SDA to make your benefit up to the basic level of £42.85 plus the age addition if you qualify for one. You can continue to receive the allowance instead of drawing your pension.

OTHER BENEFITS FOR PEOPLE WITH DISABILITIES

This section gives brief information about other benefits for people with disabilities. More detailed information is given in the leaflets mentioned or you could look at the *Disability Rights Handbook* (see page 155).

Disabled Persons Tax Credit

Disabled Persons Tax Credit (DPTC) is a tax-free, non-contributory, tax credit for disabled people who are in work but have a limited earning capacity. The Government is planning to replace DPTC with a new system of tax credits in 2003. To qualify for DPTC you will need to:

- be in paid work for at least 16 hours a week;
- be at a disadvantage in getting a job;
- be receiving or have recently received one or more of certain incapacity or disability benefits, including Incapacity Benefit, Severe Disablement Allowance and Disability Living Allowance; and
- have no more than £16,000 in savings.

If you fulfil these conditions, whether you receive DPTC, and if so how much you can get, will depend on your income and savings and factors such as the people in your family.

If you give up Incapacity Benefit or Severe Disablement Allowance in order to work and draw DPTC and the attempt at work is unsuccessful, you may be able to start drawing your previous benefit again if you claim immediately your work ceases, you are still incapable of work, and you last received your previous benefit within two years of your claim.

If you are considering giving up your disability benefit in order to work and claim DPTC, it is a good idea to seek advice first.

DPTC is administered by the Inland Revenue. Employees usually receive the credit with their wage or salary.

For more information, or to obtain the DPTC pack, ring the DPTC Helpline on 0845 60 55 858 or write to DPTC, Inland Revenue, PO Box 178, Preston PR1 0YY. Alternatively you can contact your local Inland Revenue Enquiry Centre.

Industrial injuries scheme

The industrial injuries scheme can provide help to people who are disabled as a result of an accident at work or an industrial disease. The main benefit is Disablement Benefit, which can be paid in addition to other National Insurance benefits such as Incapacity Benefit or Retirement Pension. The level of payment depends on how disabled you are assessed as being. If you are awarded Disablement Benefit at the 100 per cent rate, you may also qualify for Constant Attendance Allowance if you need care and attention. There is also an Exceptionally Severe Disablement Allowance for those who are likely to need high levels of attention on a permanent basis.

See social security leaflets SD6 (industrial diseases), SD7 (accidents at work) and DB1 (which is a more detailed guide).

War Disablement Pensions and War Widows'/Widowers' Pensions

You may be entitled to a War Disablement Pension if you are disabled as a result of war or peacetime service in the armed forces. The amount awarded depends on how disabled you are. Civilians and certain other people, such as those in the Mercantile Marines, who are disabled by an injury due to war may also qualify for a War Disablement Pension. There are extra allowances which may be paid in addition to a War Disablement Pension. These include Constant Attendance Allowance for people needing a lot of care and attention because of their pensioned disablement and a Mobility Supplement if they have difficulty walking because of that disablement.

You may be entitled to a War Widow's/Widower's Pension if you are the widow or widower of someone whose death was due to, or substantially hastened by, service in the armed forces or an injury due to war. The amount paid depends on the rank of the person who has died and the age of the widow or widower.

If you remarry, your War Widow's Pension will be withdrawn. Since 19 July 1995 a war widow who remarried but is widowed again or whose marriage has ended in divorce or judicial separation may now receive her pension again. From April 2002 this also applies to a widower's pension. The pension will normally restart from the date you claim. For a claim form or more information, ring the War Pensions Helpline on 0800 169 2277 or write to the War Pensions Agency (address on page 146).

The War Pensioners' Welfare Service has welfare officers who can offer help and advice to war pensioners and war widows who have problems about pensions or other matters. If you wish to consult a welfare officer, you should contact your nearest War Pensioners' Welfare Office. Your local social security office will give you the address or you will find it in the leaflet mentioned below. Alternatively, you can contact the War Pensions Helpline or look in your local telephone directory under 'War Pensions Agency'.

There are also a number of service organisations which can help war pensioners and war widows. Details of some of these organisations are included in the leaflet mentioned below.

See War Pensions leaflet WPA 1.

Ex-gratia payments for British groups held prisoner by the Japanese

In November 2000 the Government announced that it would make a single ex-gratia payment of £10,000 to the surviving members of British groups held prisoner by the Japanese during the Second World War. Payments will be made to:

- surviving members of the armed forces or merchant navy who were held prisoner in the Far East;
- certain former service personnel who were members of the colonial forces;
- British civilians interned in the Far East; and
- a surviving widow or widower of these groups.

Payments will not be taken into account for income-related benefits. For more information contact the War Pensions Agency at the address on page 146.

Other Financial Benefits

This part of Your Rights *gives details about other financial help that may be available for older people. It covers a variety of subjects including paying for fuel and other household bills, health costs, and paying for care – either in your own home or in a residential or nursing home.*

In some cases the financial assistance outlined depends on your income and savings or whether you are receiving another benefit such as Income Support.

HOUSEHOLD BILLS, INSULATION AND REPAIRS

This section looks at some of the main household bills and expenses that older people face. It briefly covers dealing with debt and then summarises the help that may be available for different expenses, referring you to Age Concern factsheets and other sources of information where appropriate. More detailed information is given about: paying for fuel, insulation and draughtproofing and repairs; and the Council Tax.

Difficulties with payments and dealing with debt

Many older people have to manage on low incomes and sometimes face particular problems when an unexpected bill comes in or income drops for example due to a major change such as bereavement. If you are having difficulty managing, the first thing you should do is check whether you are entitled to any additional income such as the benefits described in this book (for example Income Support, Housing Benefit or Council Tax Benefit). It may also help to make a detailed account of your income and expenditure to see if there are ways you can economise. If you have bills that you cannot pay, do not ignore them. It may be possible to come to some arrangement to make payments over a period of time. Above all, if you are worried seek help from a local advice agency. It may be able to advise you about benefit entitlement and help negotiate with your creditors.

For further information see Age Concern Books publication *Managing Debt* – see page 159.

Help with bills and expenses

Fuel: There are no regular weekly social security payments towards fuel bills but there are Winter Fuel Payments and Cold Weather Payments as described below. Grants towards insulation and draughtproofing may help you heat your home more effectively.

Rent and mortgage costs: Help towards rent comes through Housing Benefit (see pages 62–77) while homeowners may get help with their mortgage interest payments and certain service charges through Income Support (see pages 40–57). Both these benefits are based on your savings and income.

Council Tax: Council Tax Benefit (see pages 62–77) is based on income and savings. There are also other ways of reducing bills which are described on pages 118–119.

Water rates: There are no specific social security benefits to help with the cost of water rates or sewerage charges. However some water companies have charitable funds to help people in financial need. In Scotland transitional relief is available until 2004 to limit the cost of water charges for people in receipt of Council Tax Benefit. Contact your local council or water company for details.

Telephone costs: Some people who are sick or disabled may be able to receive help from their local authority social services department. However there is no national scheme providing financial help with telephone charges. See Age Concern Factsheet 28 *Help with Telephones.*

Repairs and improvements: In some situations you may be able to receive a grant to help with household repairs or improvements as explained on pages 116–118.

PAYING FOR FUEL AND INSULATION

The cost of fuel is a major expense for most pensioners. This section outlines what help is available and the different ways to pay your bills.

Fuel debts

If you cannot pay your fuel bills, you may be threatened with disconnection. However, all gas and electricity suppliers must offer special services to people of pensionable age and people with disabilities or who are chronically sick. These services include not disconnecting supplies for non-payment of bills during the winter months to households where all the occupants are pensioners. Other services that you would be entitled to are: an annual free safety check for gas customers; provision of special controls or adaptors for meters and electrical appliances; and repositioning of a meter if it would be more convenient. Let your gas or electricity supplier know that you want to register for these services.

'Fuel direct'

If you have a fuel debt and are receiving Income Support or income-based Jobseeker's Allowance (JSA), you may be able to avoid disconnection or get reconnected by going on 'fuel direct'. Some of your benefit will be withheld every week and paid direct to the company. If you think that too large an amount is being withheld, ask the local social security office which administers your Income Support whether the company will accept a smaller amount.

Winter Fuel Payments

Winter Fuel Payments started in Winter 1997–1998 to provide help with the cost of fuel bills for pensioner households. They are made to most people aged 60 or over living in Great Britain and there are no income or savings limits. The payments are based on someone's age and other circumstances in the week beginning with the third Monday in September.

In the winter of 2001–2002 the Winter Fuel Payment was £200 for eligible households and the Government has said that payments at this level will continue to be made each winter during this Parliament: thus for Winter 2002–2003, if you are aged 60 or over, you will normally receive £100 or £200, depending on your circumstances.

If you, or your partner if you have one, do not receive Income Support (or income-based Jobseeker's Allowance) you should get £200 if you are the only person in the household entitled to a payment and £100 if you share a household with one or more other people entitled to a payment – for example a married couple, or two friends living together, will each receive £100.

If you are receiving Income Support you should receive £200 regardless of who else is in the household. If you are one of a couple and your partner receives Income Support, then he or she will receive £200 on behalf of both of you and you will not get a payment.

Some people are not eligible for payments – for example people living permanently in a care home who receive Income Support and people who have been in hospital for more than 52 weeks will not get a payment. People living in a care home who are not receiving Income Support will normally receive £100.

If you are receiving a State Pension, Income Support or certain other benefits, or if you received a payment last winter, then you should not need to claim as payments will normally be made automatically before Christmas. In other circumstances – for example if you are a man aged 60 not receiving any State benefits – you will need to make a claim. The DWP runs a Winter Fuel Payment helpline which people can contact to make a claim or if they have questions about the payments. The number is 08459 15 15 15. If you need to make a claim for the payment for Winter 2002–2003, you must do this by 30 March 2003. However, there is no time limit for claims for the first three winters (ie 1997–98, 1998–99 and 1999–2000).

Cold Weather Payments

If you receive Income Support or income-based JSA and it includes a pensioner or disability premium, you may be eligible for Cold Weather Payments. A payment of £8.50 is made when the average temperature at a specified weather station has been recorded as, or is forecast to be, 0° Celsius or below over seven consecutive days. Savings are not taken into account. These payments will be made automatically so you do not have to make a claim.

Grants for energy efficiency

If you live in England the Home Energy Efficiency Scheme
(HEES) provides Warm Front grants towards energy
conservation measures. People aged 60 or over can apply for
'Warm Front Plus' grants, if they are receiving one of the
following income-related benefits: Income Support (Minimum
Income Guarantee), Housing Benefit, Council Tax Benefit or
income-based Jobseeker's Allowance. As well as offering a
range of insulation measures, they can also, where appropriate,
provide energy efficient central heating systems for the main
living areas. This should ensure that, not only is the household
warmer, but energy bills should also decrease. The maximum
Warm Front Plus grant is £2,500. The grants are targeted at
eligible owner occupiers and tenants in private rented
accommodation. In addition, in some areas those households
receiving a Warm Front Plus grant will also have an assessment
conducted on the security of their home. Where this identifies a
need for window or door locks or other similar measures, these
will also be installed.

Households with people aged 60 or over who are not eligible
for Warm Front Plus may be able to get a Warm Front grant if
they are receiving Attendance Allowance, Disability Living
Allowance or certain other disability benefits. This will provide
the same package of insulation and heating measures apart from
the electric or gas central heating. The maximum grant is
£1,000.

For more information about the grants and how to apply ring
Freephone 0800 316 6011.

If you live in Wales

The Home Energy Efficiency Scheme in Wales provides grants
for people aged 60 or over who are receiving one of the
following income-related benefits: Income Support, Housing
Benefit, Council Tax Benefit, income-based Jobseeker's
Allowance or certain disability benefits including Disability

Living Allowance or Attendance Allowance. The grant will offer a variety of insulation measures, including cavity wall and loft insulation and the installation of gas or electric central heating. The maximum grant is £1,500 (or £2,700 including gas central heating or storage heating where there is no gas supply). The National Assembly is looking at the possibility of a small-scale oil heating programme in rural Wales. Households not receiving one of the benefits outlined above but who are aged 60 or over may be entitled to a 25% grant (to a maximum of £375). For more information about the grants and how to apply ring Freephone 0800 072 0150.

If you live in Scotland

In Scotland energy grants are made under the Warm Deal scheme. The grant covers a package of energy efficiency measures, all or some of which may be offered, according to the energy needs of the home. Grants may be offered to homeowners and tenants (including council tenants) who receive any or more of the following income-related benefits: Income Support, Housing Benefit, Council Tax Benefit or certain disability benefits including Disability Living Allowance or Attendance Allowance.

The maximum grant is £500 and may cover the following energy efficiency measures: cavity wall insulation; loft insulation; draughtproofing; hot and cold tank and pipe insulation; energy advice and up to four energy efficient light bulbs. The scheme is administered by EAGA Partnership which can arrange for a registered installer to do the work. If you want to carry out the work yourself, a lower grant of up to £160 is available to cover the cost of materials, but you must not buy any materials until authorised by EAGA. Those over 60, but not in receipt of any of the benefits listed above, may qualify for a reduced grant of £125 or 25% of the cost of the work, whichever is the lower. For more information about the grants and how to apply contact the Energy Action Grants Agency (EAGA) on Freephone 0800 072 0150.

The Scottish Executive is currently working to provide free central heating for every pensioner and for all those in local authority housing in Scotland who do not currently have central heating. Work will continue on this project until 2006. Free central heating is available regardless of income or savings, and the scheme covers up to £2,500 worth of work. EAGA Partnership administers the scheme for privately rented and owner occupied housing. You can contact them on 0800 653 1653 for more details. If you live in council or housing association accommodation, your landlord will be able to give you more details about work they will do under the scheme.

For more information, contact your local energy advice centre on Freephone 0800 512 012.

For more information about all aspects of heating, including paying bills, see Age Concern Factsheet 1 *Help with Heating*.

Help with repairs and improvements

England and Wales

Homeowners and some private tenants may be able to get a 'renovation grant' towards the cost of certain repairs or improvements from their local authority. This might include installing an inside toilet or a hot and cold water supply. These grants will depend on your income and savings.

All renovation grants are discretionary. The local authority should publish a 'private sector renewal strategy' explaining who will get priority for these grants.

'Home repair assistance', which is also discretionary, is intended to cover smaller items of work such as rewiring and insulating your home or minor adaptations. It is available to owner-occupiers, private tenants or housing association tenants. Grants of up to £5,000 can be given for each application for home repair assistance in relation to any property. There is no limit on the number of applications that can be made in any period. Home repair assistance is available to anyone who is over 60 or is 'disabled or infirm' or who is receiving a means-tested benefit. Local authorities have considerable discretion in deciding who should get assistance.

'Disabled facilities grants' cover a variety of improvement and adaptation work intended to make life easier for someone with a disability. Some are mandatory and some discretionary, depending on the type of work needed. Disabled facilities grants will usually be mandatory if your home needs adaptations to enable you to get in and out of it or to use essential facilities, such as a bathroom, toilet or kitchen. They are also subject to an assessment of income and savings.

If you need help with repairs, improvements or adaptations, you should apply to the renovation grant section of your local authority. You should not start the work or buy any of the materials until you have received the local authority's approval to go ahead.

If you receive Income Support you may be able to claim a discretionary Community Care Grant or Budgeting Loan for minor household repairs (see pages 58–61).

In some areas there are home improvement agencies such as 'Care and Repair' or 'Staying Put' projects which give advice and practical assistance to homeowners needing to repair or adapt their homes. Your local authority or local Age Concern group should know whether there is a scheme in your area or contact *foundations*, the National Co-ordinating Body for Home Improvement Agencies, at the address on page 153.

See Age Concern Factsheet 13 *Older Homeowners: Financial help with repairs and adaptations.*

Scotland

In Scotland the system of grants is different and only brief information is given here. Grants may be available from the local authority housing department to owners and private tenants to help meet the cost of improvement and repair work.

Most grants are discretionary but you must be awarded a grant in some circumstances; for example if your home lacks certain standard amenities. At the time of writing the system of grants is being reviewed. You may also get help towards the costs of housing aids and adaptations if you are assessed by the social work department as needing these.

For details of grants contact your local authority housing department or obtain Age Concern Factsheet 13s (the Scottish version).

HELP WITH THE COUNCIL TAX

The Council Tax is the system of paying towards local government services in England, Scotland and Wales. The rates system continues in Northern Ireland. Under the Council Tax system all domestic dwellings are allocated to one of eight bands (A–H) depending on their estimated value in April 1991. The level of tax for a property in band H will be three times as high as the tax for a property in band A. One bill will be sent to each household. One or more people will be legally responsible for paying the bill, although the household can choose how to divide up the bill.

There are various ways that your bill may be reduced and these are summarised below. It may be possible to receive help from more than one of these schemes.

Exemptions Some properties, mainly certain empty ones, will be exempt, which means that there will be no Council Tax to pay. For example, your former home will be exempt if it is empty because you are living in a hospital or residential or nursing home, or because you have gone to live with someone else in order to receive or provide personal care. A property is also exempt if a severely mentally impaired person lives there alone and would be liable to pay the tax.

Disability reduction scheme The property may be placed in a lower band if it has certain features which are important for a disabled person such as extra space for a wheelchair or an additional bathroom or kitchen for the use of the disabled person. If your home qualifies for a reduction, your bill will be reduced to the level of tax for the band below the one your home is in. Since April 2000 properties in the lowest band (A) that have the relevant disability features have also qualified for a reduction. In this situation bills will be reduced by one sixth. Contact your local authority if you think that your property would qualify for a reduction.

Discounts The Council Tax assumes that there are two or more people living in each property. A discount of a quarter (25 per cent) will be given if someone lives alone and a discount of half (50 per cent) will normally be given if no one is living there. However, some people will not be counted for the purposes of the Council Tax so discounts may still be given even if there are two or more people in a property. For example, someone who is 'severely mentally impaired' will not be counted. The discount can also apply to a carer who lives with and, for at least 35 hours a week, is caring for someone receiving the highest care component of Disability Living Allowance or the higher rate of Attendance Allowance. You will not get this discount, however, if the person you care for is your partner or is a child under 18.

Council Tax Benefit This depends on the income and savings of the person(s) responsible for the bill or the people they live with. It is described in more detail on pages 62–77.

For further information see Age Concern Factsheet 21 *The Council Tax and Older People.*

PAYING FOR CARE

This section explains the help you can get with paying for the costs of care in all settings. This might be care at home (such as personal care or domestic help in your home, day care or a night sitting service) or care in a care home. It covers people living in England, Scotland and Wales. Although the system in Northern Ireland is broadly similar, there are some differences, so contact Age Concern Northern Ireland if you need more information.

Many people buy their own care without social services help. This section looks at the help you can receive from social services and how you may be charged for that help. There are national rules for charging for care in care homes but each local authority is able to decide whether and how much to charge for care to help you remain at home.

Applying for help with care

If you need help with your care, either to help you to remain at home or if you think you might need to move into a care home, you can ask for an assessment of your needs by the local authority (the county, metropolitan or London Borough or unitary authority). The social services department (social work department in Scotland) will be responsible for arranging an assessment of your care needs. After this assessment it will decide whether it can offer you any help either to enable you to stay at home or in a care home. Each local authority has its own criteria for making these decisions. Some local authorities have a ceiling on the amount (either the number of hours or the cost) of care it will provide to help you remain at home. If you do not agree with its decision you can make a complaint through the complaints procedure.

Since April 2001 your carer (if you have one) has also been entitled to an assessment in their own right and to services that will help them care for you. They have a right to an assessment even if you do not want to be assessed.

PAYING FOR CARE AT HOME

This section looks at the help you can receive either from local authorities through Direct Payments or from the Independent Living Fund in paying for care to help you remain at home. It then explains the rules that local authorities use when working out how much to charge you for care it has provided or arranged for you.

Direct payments

Local authorities can give people cash payments as an alternative to directly arranging community care services. These payments were originally only available to people who qualified before the age of 65 but the rules changed in 2000 so that people aged 65 and over can now apply. You can choose to employ a carer yourself, or use a local home care agency if you do not wish to take on the responsibility of being an employer. You may find that there is a support group in your area to help people with managing direct payments. Carers are also able to receive direct payments instead of services which can be provided for them.

To get a direct payment you have to be able to manage the payments (alone or with assistance). They cannot be used to pay a spouse or close relative in the same household. The local authority has to monitor that the money is being spent on the care you need. Not all local authorities have direct payment schemes at the moment but they may be made mandatory. If you want a direct payment but your local authority does not run a scheme or refuses on other grounds you can use the complaints procedure.

Direct payments are available to people with care needs in Scotland, and from the start of 2003 they will be available as of right to any community care user who wants to use them. For more details of direct payments, call the direct payments helpline on 0131 558 3450.

For more information about direct payments in your area, contact your local authority. See also Age Concern Factsheet 24 *Direct Payments from Social Services*.

The Independent Living Fund (ILF)

The Independent Living (Extension) Fund makes payments to people already receiving help at the end of March 1993. The Independent Living (1993) Fund makes payments to new applicants. Both provide cash payments to enable severely disabled people to pay for personal care or help with household tasks in order to remain living at home.

You can be considered for help from the discretionary Independent Living (1993) Fund only if you are under the age of 66. You must also be receiving the highest care component of Disability Living Allowance, have no more than £18,500 in savings (although this limit may increase), be receiving Income Support or income-based JSA or not be able to afford the care you need from your income, and be receiving services or cash from the local authority, currently to the value of at least £200 a week. The maximum weekly payment from the ILF is normally £375.

For more information about the Independent Living (1993) Fund contact your local authority social services department.

Charges for care at home

Each local authority has discretion whether it will charge people who receive care either from or arranged by the local authority. Very few authorities do not charge anything. Any services arranged under Section 117 of the Mental Health Act for aftercare following detention in hospital must be free (however in Scotland the different laws mean that these services are chargeable). Any services arranged by the NHS, such as visits by the district nurse, are also free.

However any charge you do pay must be 'reasonable' for you to pay, and you have the right to ask the local authority to reduce the amount or waive it altogether. It is important that the local authority is aware if you have extra costs because of your disability, such as having to pay for a gardener or someone to clean the house, or taxis because you cannot use public transport. Any charge should only be based on your resources. If you disagree with your charge you can use the local authority's complaints procedure.

The Department of Health has issued guidance setting out a framework which local authorities must use when they decide their policies. By April 2003, the charging policies of all local authorities in England will have to be in line with the guidance. There will also be guidance in Wales and Scotland.

See Age Concern Factsheet 6 *Finding Help at Home* and Factsheet 46 *Paying for Help at Home and Local Authority Charges*.

Short breaks

If the local authority arranges short periods in a care home it can charge in one of two ways as long as the stay is less than eight weeks. It can either choose to have a 'set' charge which must be reasonable, or it can use the means test used to calculate the charge for care homes (see below). The value of your home will be ignored as it counts as a temporary stay. If your care break is in hospital or arranged by the NHS it will be free. Benefits may be affected depending on how frequent your care is and how long it lasts.

PAYING FOR CARE IN A CARE HOME

This section summarises the help you can get with care home charges. The term 'care home' covers all homes that are registered homes under the Care Standards Act 2000. This includes independent homes and those owned by the local authority and which provide personal and/or nursing care.

Before the local authority can offer any financial help you need to have an assessment of your needs as described on pages 120–121. Please note also that the information in this section does not apply to people whose care is in a home which provides nursing care which has been arranged and fully paid for by the NHS and who are regarded as long-stay NHS patients, nor to those who receive their care free under Section 117 of the Mental Health Act (the rules are different in Scotland).

In England and Wales the NHS is responsible for the funding of care provided by a registered nurse in a care home providing nursing care for all those who fund their own care. This means that this part of your care will be free. In Scotland from July 2002 it is expected that the Scottish Executive, through local authorities, will cover the cost of personal and nursing care and individuals will make payments to cover accommodation costs.

For more information about the level of funding you are likely to receive towards your nursing care, see Age Concern Factsheet 20 *NHS Continuing Care, Free Nursing Care and Intermediate Care*, or contact Age Concern England, Scotland or Cymru at the addresses on page 157.

From April 2002 there have been some major changes to the financial support you get from the Department for Work and Pensions and it may vary depending on whether you were already receiving Income Support by 8 April 2002. These changes are explained in the text below which also explains the rules for charges. Until April 2002 people who had been in a care home since before 1 April 1993 were entitled to special higher levels of Income Support known as 'preserved rights'. This system has been abolished and the local authority charging procedure now applies to everyone including those who have been in a home since before 1 April 1993. This section also includes details about when Attendance Allowance or Disability Living Allowance (DLA) can be paid.

You should be aware that although there are national assessment and charging procedures, sometimes things do not run as smoothly as described here. For example there may be delays in obtaining an assessment or the local authority may not agree to take financial responsibility. If you have problems a local advice agency may be able to help.

Care arranged by the local authority

If the local authority agrees to arrange a place for you in a private or voluntary care home, it will be responsible for paying the full fee to the home and assessing your income and savings to work out how much you must pay towards the fees. If you are in a local authority home, the local authority uses the same rules to work out how much you should pay towards the cost of providing the home. If you wish, you will be able to choose a different home (subject to certain conditions). If the home you choose is more expensive than the local authority thinks you need, then the local authority will arrange this as long as there is someone (such as a friend, relative or charity) able to make up the difference. You cannot use your own money to make up the difference, unless you are in the period of the 12 week disregard of the property, or have entered into a deferrred payment agreement (see page 127).

If there is no suitable place at the price the local authority would usually pay for someone with your assessed needs, it will be responsible for paying for a more expensive place to meet your needs.

Charging procedures

If you have more than £19,000 savings, you will have to pay the full fee until your savings reach £19,000. If you are already in a home and are using up your savings, you should apply to the local authority for help a few months before your savings get down to £19,000. (See pages 126–128 for how your former home is treated.) This figure of £19,000 (and the figure of £11,750 below) was included in a Department of Health consultation paper, but you should note that at the time of writing (March 2002) it had not been confirmed.

If you have £16,000 or less, you may be able to receive Income Support as well as financial support from the local authority towards the fees. If you are already in a home, apply for Income Support as soon as your savings reach £16,000. The savings limits for the Income Support and local authority financial assessments used to be the same but this is no longer the case. For the local authority assessment, savings of £11,750 or less will be ignored; savings between £11,750 and £19,000 will be counted as though you have an additional £1 a week income from every £250 (or part of £250) over £11,750. This is called 'tariff income'. For Income Support, tariff income is assessed for savings between £10,000 and £16,000.

For Income Support your income will be assessed as described on pages 43–45. Your applicable amount will be calculated as on pages 45–49, if you apply for Income Support from 8 April 2002. If you were already receiving Income Support in an independent home before that date, an additional 'Residential Allowance' of £71.65 a week for homes in Greater London and £64.40 for homes elsewhere is paid. If you were receiving Income Support in a local authority home before 8 April 2002, you will continue just to have your income made up to the Basic State Pension of £75.50. Any absences from the home could mean that your benefits will be calculated under the new rules for those applying for Income Support from 8 April 2002.

The local authority also assesses your income and savings. From your assessed income (including tariff income), you will have to make a contribution towards the fees which will leave you with at least £16.80 a week for personal expenses. However, this figure of £16.80 is the one used in consultation and at the time of writing had not been confirmed.

Owning your home
Local authority assessment

If you are in a local authority home or the local authority has arranged a place in a private or voluntary home and you own your own home, its value will normally be taken into account, unless your stay is only temporary, or your partner lives there, a child under 16 for whom you are responsible, or a 'relative' who is either disabled or aged 60 or over lives there. In addition, since April 2001 you normally have a 12-week period when the value of the home will be ignored from the time you become a permanent resident. This is on top of any disregard while your stay was considered temporary.

The local authority can also choose to ignore the value of your home if someone else lives there, for instance a friend aged over 60, or a relative or friend under 60 who has been caring for you for a substantial period. If the local authority says it will not use this discretion, you might want to complain through the formal complaints procedure.

If the local authority does not ignore the value of your former home, it will be able to place a 'charge' on its value, so that it can reclaim money owed to it when the property is sold. You should seek legal advice about this. Since October 2001 local authorities have been given an extra grant to help them offer more legal charges and not to put pressure on residents to sell their homes. Instead you can enter into a 'deferred payment agreement' with the local authority.

For details about who counts as a relative in this situation and further information about the treatment of the former home, see Age Concern Factsheet 38 *Treatment of the Former Home as Capital for People in Care Homes.*

The local authority will also be able to take account of certain assets which you might have transferred to someone else in order to pay less for your care. It may be able to recover any debt from the recipients of such assets if the transfer was made within six months of the local authority arranging the funding of the place in the home. Even if the transfer was made more than six months before, the asset can still be taken into account. Further information is available in Age Concern Factsheet 40 *Transfer of Assets and Paying for Care in a Care Home.*

Income Support assessment

If you own your own home its value will normally be taken into account when your savings are assessed for Income Support.

However, this value will be ignored for 26 weeks, or longer if reasonable, if you are taking steps to sell it. The value of your home will also be ignored if your spouse or partner lives there, or a 'relative' who is either disabled or aged 60 or over lives in the property.

For details about the system for people in local authority homes or needing local authority support in private or voluntary homes after 1 April 1993, see Age Concern Factsheet 10 *Local Authority Charging Procedures for Care Homes.*

Couples

When one of a couple enters a care home, the local authority will assess the amount that the resident has to pay towards the fees solely on the resident's income and savings. However, a spouse is considered to be a 'liable relative', which means that they may have an obligation to contribute towards the cost of care. An unmarried partner has no liability under the local authority charging procedures to pay for a partner's care.

The local authority has no power to insist on a means test of your spouse and, although some authorities may have developed their own formulae, there are no specific national rules about how much your spouse must pay. A spouse can be invited to make a contribution, and a voluntary agreement may be reached.

If no voluntary agreement is reached, the local authority can make a complaint to a Magistrates' Court (Sheriff Court in Scotland), which has the power to decide how much, if anything, a liable relative should pay.

If you have an occupational or personal pension and your spouse is not also living in a care home with you, the local authority will ignore half the pension when assessing your income if you pass at least this amount to your spouse.

The local authority can also use its discretion to vary the amount of the personal expenses allowance. For example, you might want to ask for this to be done if you are not married to your partner, as the local authority will not automatically ignore half of your pension in this situation.

The person at home may be able to claim benefits such as Income Support in their own right, depending on their income and savings.

See Age Concern Factsheet 39 *Paying for a Care Home if you have a Partner.*

Attendance Allowance or Disability Living Allowance in a care home

The mobility component of Disability Living Allowance (DLA) is not affected by admission to a care home.

Whether or not you can receive Attendance Allowance or the care component of DLA will depend on how the fees are being met.

If you are paying the full charges in a private or voluntary home or a local authority home, you can claim and receive Attendance Allowance or DLA provided you fulfil the other conditions (see pages 80–82 and 83–85). You can receive these allowances whether you arranged the admission yourself or the local authority arranged the admission. The fact that the NHS pays for your nursing care in a home providing nursing does not affect your ability to receive Attendance Allowance or DLA. Only if the NHS pays for the full fees will your Attendance Allowance or DLA be affected as you will be regarded as a hospital inpatient (see page 86).

If you need local authority financial support in order to meet the home's fees, you cannot start to receive Attendance Allowance or the care component of DLA. If you are already receiving one of these allowances, it will stop four weeks after the admission.

However, you may still retain an 'underlying entitlement' to the allowance, so that if, for example you move out of the home, you could start receiving the allowance again without making a fresh claim. You should contact the social security office and ask for the allowance to be paid again. Recent cases have established that if the local authority temporarily provides funding but is later reimbursed by the resident, Attendance Allowance or the care component of DLA is payable for that period as long as Income Support is not in payment. Get advice if your Attendance Allowance and DLA has been stopped and you do not think that it should have been, or contact Age Concern England at the address on page 157 for more information.

You may be able to receive one of these allowances if you claim Income Support as long as the local authority is not funding the fees in any way. The rules on this are different in Scotland so this applies only in England and Wales. For more information about payment of Attendance Allowance in care homes contact Age Concern England at the address on page 157 for a paper called *Attendance Allowance in Care Homes*.

Changes in Scotland from July 2002

In Scotland, people in care homes will no longer be able to receive Attendance Allowance or the care component of DLA once free personal care is introduced (probably in July 2002). The Scottish Executive payments made through local authorities for personal care will take into account the loss of these allowances.

HELP WITH HEALTH COSTS

Most of the treatment given under the National Health Service (NHS) is free, but there are some things for which most people have to pay part or all of the cost. This section first outlines hearing and chiropody services, which are free under the NHS. It then explains who can get help with the cost of other NHS services such as dental care, eye tests and glasses.

Free NHS services

Hearing aids

You should discuss hearing difficulties with your GP who may, if necessary, refer you to a hospital for tests. If you are prescribed a hearing aid, this will be fitted and issued by a local NHS hearing aid centre. NHS hearing aids are available on free loan; replacements and batteries are also free. It is possible to buy private hearing aids, but these can be expensive and are not necessarily more effective.

The Royal National Institute for Deaf People (RNID) produces a range of information leaflets on hearing loss, hearing aids and other matters concerning deafness – see address on page 154.

Chiropody

NHS chiropody services are free to those with a clinical need but there is some variation in the extent of the provision. To find out about your local NHS chiropody service, ask at your GP's surgery or telephone NHS Direct on 0845 46 47 (24 hours). All chiropodists employed in the NHS are state registered.

If you wish to consider private treatment your local NHS chiropody service may have details. Alternatively you may wish to refer to *Yellow Pages*.

Help with NHS costs

If you (or your partner if you have one) receive Income Support or income-based Jobseeker's Allowance (JSA), you are entitled to receive help with the health costs described below by showing your order book or a letter from the social security office. If you receive Disabled Persons Tax Credit (DPTC), you may also get this help depending on the level of your award. In the following paragraphs, wherever Income Support is mentioned it also covers these other benefits. In certain circumstances help may also be available to people receiving a war pension.

If you are not entitled to help through getting Income Support, DPTC or income-based JSA but have no more than £12,000 (£8,000 if you are aged under 60) in savings, you can apply for help with health costs under the NHS Low Income Scheme. (The limit for people living permanently in care homes is different – £18,500 in March 2002, although this may change in April.) If you qualify you will be sent one of two certificates. Certificate HC 2 entitles you to full help with health costs. If your income is a little higher, you may get certificate HC 3, which entitles you to partial help with health costs. The certificates tell you how long they last. If you are aged 60 or over, the certificate will normally last for 12 months. To apply for a certificate under the Low Income Scheme, you can get form HC 1 from your local social security office or NHS hospital; some dentists, opticians and GP surgeries also have them. (If you live permanently in a care home and receive financial support from the local authority, ask the owner of the home for form HC 1 (SC).) It is best to apply in advance. Remember that if you receive Income Support, you do not need to apply for a certificate.

See Department of Health leaflet HC 11.

Prescriptions

NHS prescriptions are free to people aged 60 or over. However, younger people can also get free prescriptions if they have a low income or suffer from one of a small number of 'specified medical conditions', which are listed in leaflet HC 11.

Prescriptions are free to people receiving Income Support and those who have certificate HC 2 on grounds of low income, as described above. People who have certificate HC 3 entitling them to partial help with some NHS costs cannot get help towards prescription charges.

If you cannot get free prescriptions, you may be able to save money by buying a prepayment certificate or 'season ticket'. The application form FP95 is available from main post offices, pharmacists and health authorities.

Dental care

NHS dental treatment, check-ups and dentures are free if you or your partner gets Income Support or if you have certificate HC 2. The cost may be reduced if you have certificate HC 3. Details of how to apply for a certificate are given above. Every time you start a new course of treatment, tell the dentist that you are on Income Support or have certificate HC2 or HC3.

Unless you are entitled to free treatment or help with the costs, you will have to pay 80 per cent of the cost of most treatment up to a maximum of £366 in England and Scotland, and £354 in Wales for one course of treatment.

It is a good idea to make sure that you are registered with an NHS dentist for regular treatment (called 'continuing care'), as this means that you will be entitled under the NHS to any treatment that the dentist considers necessary to secure and maintain your oral health. Contact NHS Direct on 0845 46 47 for advice on how to find an NHS dentist. Its number will be in the phone book.

● **No help is given towards private dental fees. If you want NHS dental care, make sure the dentist is providing you with NHS treatment before you start each course. You can do this when you discuss the proposed treatment with your dentist.**

See Age Concern Factsheet 5 *Dental Care and Older People.*

Sight tests and glasses

Sight tests are available free to all people aged 60 or over. Younger people will also qualify for a free NHS sight test if they or their partner receives Income Support or has certificate HC 2 as described above. Free tests are also available to people who belong to a priority group, which includes registered blind and partially sighted people, those who need complex lenses, and diagnosed diabetics. People who have glaucoma or someone aged 40 or over who is the parent, brother, sister or son or daughter of a person with diagnosed glaucoma will also qualify.

If you cannot get to the optician's practice for a sight test, you may be able to arrange for an optician to visit you at home. If you are entitled to a free NHS sight test, you will not have to pay for the visit.

You are entitled to a voucher towards the cost of glasses provided you or your partner gets Income Support or has certificate HC 2. You may get some help if you have certificate HC 3. You may be able to claim a refund in some circumstances if you do not receive your certificate in time, but it is better to apply well in advance. The voucher carries a financial value linked to your optical prescription; it may cover the full cost of the glasses or be used as part payment for a more expensive pair. If your glasses or contact lenses cost more than any voucher you are given, you will have to pay the difference. If you need complex lenses, you will be able to receive a voucher from your optician to help pay for the glasses regardless of income and savings. However, the amount of help will be greater if you or your partner receives Income Support or qualifies on grounds of low income.

You do not have to get your glasses from the optician who does your sight test, although you may choose to do so. If you prefer to obtain your glasses from a different optician, simply take your prescription to them.

Before you have a sight test or get glasses, find out whether you qualify for help. If you will have to pay for some or all of the cost, it is best to 'shop around' to check whether another optician might be cheaper, as charges can vary.

People with serious eye conditions and who require specialist hospital care only have to pay up to a maximum charge and the hospital then meets the difference between the maximum charge and the cost of the glasses.

Elastic hosiery, wigs, fabric supports

Elastic support stockings are available on prescription, and are free to both men and women aged 60 or over. Support tights are usually available only through the hospital service, and there may be a charge for these. However, they will be provided free of charge if you receive Income Support or have certificate HC 2.

Wigs and fabric supports are supplied through hospitals and are free for in-patients. If you are an out-patient, there are charges depending on the type of wig or fabric support supplied. However, they are free if you are on Income Support or have certificate HC 2; if you have certificate HC 3, you may get some help with the cost.

Hospital travel costs

If you get Income Support, you are entitled to help with the necessary costs of travelling to and from hospital for NHS treatment. You may also get help towards these costs if you have certificate HC 2 or HC 3 on grounds of low income. See 'Help with NHS costs' above on how to apply for a certificate. If you are not sure what help you can get, contact the hospital before you travel. Hospitals will not normally reimburse taxi fares unless taxis are the only transport available – check with the hospital first.

If you are visiting a close relative in hospital and you are receiving Income Support, you may be able to get help with the cost of your fares from the Social Fund (see pages 58–61).

Health care outside the UK

You are covered by the NHS only while you are in the UK. If you are abroad and fall ill, you may have to pay all or part of the cost of any treatment. There are special arrangements with European Union (EU) and some other countries which may enable you to get free or reduced cost *emergency* medical care during a visit abroad. If you are going to live in another country, you should find out well in advance about your entitlement to medical treatment there.

Before going abroad, get leaflet T6 *Health Advice for Travellers* from the local post office or by telephoning the Health Literature line (Freephone 0800 555 777) to find out what cover there might be for treatment in the country you are visiting.

This leaflet also contains general guidance on immunisation requirements for travellers. You are entitled to typhoid, polio and hepatitis A vaccines on the NHS: their administration is free and prescription charges follow the patient's normal entitlement (free for people aged 60 and over, for example). However, prescription is at the GP's discretion. All other travel immunisations are non-NHS and are likely to incur a variable charge.

It is advisable to take out private medical insurance to cover the full cost of any treatment you may need abroad whether you are going to an EU or non-EU country. Medical treatment is very expensive, as is the cost of bringing a person back to the UK in the event of illness or death.

● **No matter where you are going, check that you have enough travel insurance to cover any emergency expenses you may have to meet.**

For further information on reciprocal health care arrangements, write to the Department of Health, International and Constitutional Branch, Room 512, Richmond House, 79 Whitehall, London SW1A 2NL.

TRAVEL AND OTHER CONCESSIONS

TRAVEL

Rail and underground

All rail companies give one-third reductions on most types of ticket to people who have a Senior Railcard, which currently costs £18 (March 2002) and is valid for one year. It is available to people aged 60 or over, provided proof of age is given. Senior Railcard users can also buy a Rail Senior Card (costing £12) for savings of up to 25% on cross border rail travel in Europe. Principal stations and travel centres should have the details of how to apply for these Railcards.

If you are disabled, you can buy a Disabled Person's Railcard, which currently costs £14, and which allows you and a companion to travel at a third off most standard fares. Full details of who qualifies are given in a leaflet available from many local railway stations.

Underground or other transport systems may also offer concessions; you should ask at local offices.

Bus and coach services

In England, there is a national minimum bus concession scheme. While some local authorities may offer better concessions, all authorities must offer a minimum concession of half fare, for travel after 9.30 am, for all people of pension age or over (60 for women, 65 for men). At the time of writing legislation is being considered by Parliament to enable men to qualify for the concession at the age of 60. The change is likely to come into force in April 2003. Travel is limited to within the issuing local authority but some local neighbouring authorities have joint arrangements.

In Scotland, pensioners will be entitled to free off-peak bus travel from October 2002. Ages are expected to be equalised at 60 by April 2003.

In Wales, free bus passes for pensioners were introduced in April 2001, and from April 2002 all pensioners in Wales will have free local bus travel within their own local authority. Ages are expected to be equalised at 60 by April 2003.

Apply to your local authority (London or metropolitan borough, district council or unitary authority) for details.

National Express offers up to 30% off many standard fares for holders of the Senior Discount Coach Card. This card is available to anyone aged 50 and over and costs £9 a year (March 2002). A three-year card that costs £19 is also available. The discounts are offered on all National Express coach services within England, Scotland and Wales. Details of these concessions are obtainable from any appointed National Express agent. Other coach operators will also give concessions, but may have different age limits.

Taxicard schemes

Some local authorities operate Taxicard schemes which provide reduced fares for disabled people. Contact your local authority to find out if it runs a scheme.

Airlines

Some airlines may have concessionary fares for pensioners. Ask at the airline or travel agent for details.

See Age Concern Factsheet 26 *Travel Information for Older People.*

OTHER CONCESSIONS

People over a certain age or who are entitled to a State Pension may be able to receive concessions such as: reductions at leisure centres and swimming pools; lower admission prices to museums or other places of interest; or reduced fees for joining adult education classes. Most national museums are free for people aged 60 or over. Sometimes local businesses such as hairdressers may have special rates at certain times of the week. These concessions vary, so look out for any reductions that might apply to you.

Television licences

Television licences are free for households with a person aged 75 and over. For more information, contact the TV licensing information helpline on 0845 602 3334.

There are two other types of concession. People who are registered blind can obtain a 50% reduction from the full licence fee. It is also possible to get specially adapted TV sound receivers and these do not need a licence to operate. Some people over the age of 60 who live in care homes or certain local authority or housing association sheltered accommodation qualify for a concessionary £5 licence.

See Age Concern England Factsheet 3 *Television Licence Concessions*.

Proof of eligibility

If you are drawing a pension but do not have a pension book (for example because your pension is paid into a bank account), you can get a card proving that you are a pensioner. Write, quoting your pension number, to the Pensions and Overseas Benefits Directorate, Tyneview Park, Whitley Road, Benton, Newcastle Upon Tyne NE98 1BA. If you have no proof of being a pensioner, you may have to produce a copy of your birth certificate or another official document showing your age.

HELP FROM CHARITIES OR BENEVOLENT FUNDS

It may be possible to receive financial assistance from a charity or benevolent fund in the form of either a single payment for a specific item or regular weekly payments. Charities which make such payments will expect you first to check that you cannot receive help from other sources such as the social security system. Often benevolent funds help people in particular circumstances. For example these might be based on: the occupation (or former occupation) of the applicant or their partner; certain health problems or disabilities; the parish where the applicant lives; the type of education they had; or the fact that they had undertaken voluntary work in the community. Others may help people who are members of particular institutions or religions or organisations such as trade unions.

To find out more information you could contact a local advice agency or consult the following publications which should be available in your local library: *Charities Digest* published (in association with the Family Welfare Association) by Waterlow Professional Publishing, Paulton House, 8 Shepherdess Walk, London N1 7LB and *A Guide to Grants for Individuals in Need* published by the Directory of Social Change, 24 Stephenson Way, London NW1 2DP.

There are also two national organisations – The Association of Charity Officers (incorporating the Occupational Benevolent Funds Alliance) and Charity Search – that can help put people in contact with charities and benevolent funds. Their addresses are on page 152.

LEGAL FEES, WILLS AND FUNERALS

Help with legal costs and making wills

If you need help with a legal problem you may be able to obtain this free from a local advice agency or you may be able to get help with the cost of a solicitor's fees through the Community Legal Service run by the Legal Services Commission.

If you are on Income Support or income-based Jobseeker's Allowance or have a low income and little or no savings, you may be able to obtain help with legal advice and representation through the different schemes. This can include help with making a will but in England and Wales you must be 70 or over or mentally or physically disabled in order to receive help.

For further information see Age Concern Factsheet 43 *Obtaining and Paying for Legal Advice* and Factsheet 7 *Making Your Will*. See also *A Practical Guide to Legal Service Funding*, available from the Legal Services Commission, 85 Grays Inn Road, London WC1X 8TX. Tel: 0845 3000 343. The Scottish Legal Aid Board also publishes helpful leaflets on Legal Aid. Its address is 44 Drumsheugh Gardens, Edinburgh EH3 7SW. Tel: 0131 226 7061.

Help with funeral payments

This section describes the funeral payments available from the Social Fund which are part of the social security system. For more details about arranging a funeral, including information about the duty of local and health authorities to pay for certain funerals, see Age Concern Factsheet 27 *Arranging a Funeral*.

You may be able to receive a Social Fund Funeral Payment towards the cost of a funeral if you have good reason for taking responsibility for the expenses and you or your partner is receiving Income Support, Housing Benefit, Council Tax Benefit, income-based Jobseeker's Allowance or Disabled Person's Tax Credit. Any savings you have will not be taken into account (this applies since October 2001). However, as explained below, there are restrictions on who can receive a payment and limits on the amount of the payment so it is important to check what you are entitled to before making the arrangements.

To receive a payment you should be the partner or close relative of the person who has died, or someone else who it is reasonable to expect to take responsibility for arranging the funeral. The person who died must have been resident in the UK and usually the funeral must take place in the UK.

However, unless you are the partner of the person who has died, the social security decision maker may decide that it was not reasonable for you to have taken responsibility for the funeral costs. There may, for example, be another close relative who is not receiving a qualifying benefit.

The payment can cover necessary burial and cremation costs, certain necessary travel expenses and up to £600 for other funeral expenses.

Although your savings do not affect your entitlement to a funeral payment, if there is money available from the estate of the person who has died, or money from insurance policies or pre-paid funeral plans, this will be taken into account.

To make a claim you will need form SF 200 from your local social security office. You normally have to claim within three months of the funeral, but it is advisable to check what you are entitled to before arranging a funeral.

See social security leaflet D 49 for what to do after a death and Age Concern Factsheet 27 *Arranging a Funeral*.

Further Information

This part of Your Rights *gives details about local and national sources of help to contact for assistance and advice. In addition, there is information about obtaining Department of Work and Pensions (DWP) social security leaflets, Age Concern factsheets, and other publications on social security benefits mentioned in the book. Also included is an index to help you find the information you require in this book and a summary of the main benefit rates.*

DEPARTMENT FOR WORK AND PENSIONS

Much of the information in *Your Rights* covers State pensions and social security benefits. The Government department responsible is the Department for Work and Pensions (DWP). It replaced the Department of Social Security (DSS) in 2001. The rules for State Pensions and benefits and the levels of payment are set out in legislation – for example, each year regulations are agreed in Parliament setting out the annual increases to pensions and benefits.

Major changes are taking place to the way that pensions and benefits are administered. In April 2002 the Benefits Agency and Employment Service were replaced by the Pension Service and Jobcentre Plus. The Pension Service is responsible for pensions and benefits for older people and for providing information about pensions to people of working age. Jobcentre Plus deals with people of working age by administering social security benefits and providing advice and support about employment.

The Pension Service will have a local service, providing personal contact and working in partnership with other local organisations. This will be supported by 26 pension centres which will eventually replace the current service provided by local social security offices. You will be able to contact your nearest pension centre by telephone, letter, email, personal visit to a local venue, or through home visits – depending on your preference and personal circumstances. The new service is rolling out from April 2002 and will extend into new areas over the next few years until it covers all of England, Scotland and Wales. If you are already a pensioner and have not yet received a letter from the DWP about these changes, then continue to deal with your local social security office where the Pension Service will be operating from. If your Retirement Pension is paid direct into your bank or building society account, you should continue to deal with Pensions Direct in your usual way.

For further information call 0845 731 3233 (textphone users should call 0845 604 0210) and ask for the DWP leaflet called *The Pension Service: A guide to our new service*. For details about your local office, check in the phone book under 'Jobcentre Plus', 'Social Security Office' or 'Benefits Agency'; or ask at your local library or advice agency.

Problems with administration

If you have a problem with the administration of a benefit – for example there is a delay in processing your claim – you can contact the Pension Service. Social security leaflet GL 22 *Tell Us Your Comments and Complaints* tells you how to complain or make comments on the service you receive. If you are still dissatisfied, get in touch with a local advice agency or your MP.

National DWP addresses

Pensions and Overseas Benefits Directorate
Tyneview Park
Whitley Road
Benton
Newcastle Upon Tyne
NE98 1BA

For help and advice about the State Retirement Pension or Widow's and Bereavement Benefits paid by automated credit transfer (ACT), telephone 0191 203 0203, 7.00am–7.00pm weekdays. Textphone for the deaf or hard of hearing 0191 201 0194.

For information about benefits payable abroad, telephone 0191 218 7777, 8.00am–4.30pm weekdays. Textphone for the deaf or hard of hearing 0191 218 7280.

Disability Benefits Unit
Warbreck House
Warbreck Hill Road
Blackpool FY2 0ZG
Tel: 0845 7123456
Textphone: 0845 7224433
7.30am–6.30pm weekdays

The Disability Benefits Unit administers Disability Living Allowance and Attendance Allowance, although initial claims are normally dealt with at the regionally based Disability Benefit Centres.

Invalid Care Allowance Unit
Palatine House
Lancaster Road
Preston
Lancashire PR1 1HB
Tel: 01253 856123

Benefit Enquiry Line for people with disabilities

For advice and information about disability benefits telephone 0800 88 22 00 (a free call), 8.30am–6.30pm weekdays, 9.00am–1.00pm Saturdays. Textphone (for deaf people) 0800 24 33 55.

Staff can arrange for help with completing forms over the phone for benefits such as Attendance Allowance and Disability Living Allowance.

War Pensions Helpline

War Pensions Agency
Norcross
Blackpool FY5 3WP

For general advice on war pensions telephone 0800 169 2277 (a free call), 8.15am–5.15 pm Mondays to Thursdays, 8.15am–4.30pm Fridays.

DWP Website

If you have access to the Internet, you can obtain leaflets, publications and other information from the DWP Website. You can also download claim forms for many benefits.

Website: www.dwp.gov.uk

AGE CONCERN INFORMATION LINE

Age Concern Information Line provides a service to older people and their relatives and friends and to carers and professionals. Contact the Line (Freephone 0800 00 99 66) to obtain the factsheets listed below (up to five are available free). The factsheets include details of the telephone number to contact if you need further information. People who live in Scotland will be sent factsheets that cover Scottish law and practice where this is different.

Community care

6 Finding Help at Home
10 Local Authority Charging Procedures for Care Homes
24 Direct Payments from Social Services
29 Finding Care Home Accommodation
32 Disability and Ageing: Your rights to social services
37 Hospital Discharge Arrangements
38 Treatment of the Former Home as Capital for People in Care Homes
39 Paying for Care in a Care Home if you have a Partner
41 Local Authority Assessment for Community Care Services
46 Paying for Help at Home and Local Authority Charges

Health

5 Dental Care and Older People
20 NHS Continuing Care, Free Nursing Care and Intermediate Care
23 Help with Incontinence
44 Family Doctors and their Services
45 Fitness for Later Life

Housing

1 Help with Heating
2 Retirement Housing for Sale

For up to five free factsheets telephone 0800 00 99 66
(7 am – 7 pm, seven days a week, every day of the year).
Alternatively you may prefer to write to:

Age Concern
FREEPOST (SWB 30375)
Ashburton
Devon TQ13 7ZZ

For professionals working with older people, the
factsheets are available on an annual subscription service,
which includes updates throughout the year. For further
details and costs of the subscription, please write to
Age Concern at the above Freepost address.

LOCAL SOURCES OF HELP

Age Concern

Most areas have a local Age Concern which provides services and advice. You can find the address from the phone book, library or Citizens Advice Bureau, or you can write to the appropriate national Age Concern (addresses on page 157) for the address of your nearest group.

Citizens Advice Bureau (CAB)

The local offices provide advice and information on all kinds of subjects including social security benefits, housing and consumer problems. You can find out where your nearest CAB is from the phone book or at your local library.

Law centre

There may be a law centre giving free legal advice in your area. Check in the telephone book or at a Citizens Advice Bureau, or telephone the Law Centres Federation (020 7387 8570) or look at its Website at www.lawcentres.org.uk.

Local authority/council

In England the structure of local government depends on whether you live in a county, or in a metropolitan or London borough or a unitary authority. All areas in Scotland and Wales have a unitary authority. In England, if you live in a county, the district council will deal with Housing Benefit, Council Tax Benefit and other matters to do with the Council Tax. You will need to contact the county council about social services. In a metropolitan or London borough or unitary authority, there will be just one authority that will deal with the Council Tax, Housing Benefit and social services. Some authorities have welfare rights workers to advise on benefits. You will find the address of your local authority in the telephone book under the name of your county, unitary authority, metropolitan or London borough, or ask at your local library.

Local councillor

A councillor for your area may be able to help with problems with the local authority. You can get the names of the councillors for your 'ward' from the town hall, library or Citizens Advice Bureau.

Local Government Ombudsman

If you feel you have suffered because of maladministration in the way the local authority has dealt with your case, you can make a complaint to the Local Government Ombudsman. You can do this direct or through your local councillor. Ask a local advice agency or councillor for further information.

Member of Parliament (MP)

Your MP may be able to help with problems involving Government departments. If you do not know who your MP is, ask at the town hall, library or CAB. Most MPs hold regular surgeries locally; or you can write to your MP at the House of Commons, London SW1A 0AA. For a complaint about unfair treatment by a Government department (for example a delay with a benefit claim), ask the MP to refer your complaint to the Parliamentary Ombudsman.

In Scotland you can also contact Members of the Scottish Parliament at Scottish Parliament, Edinburgh EH99 1SP. In Wales you can contact Assembly Members at the National Assembly for Wales, Cardiff Bay, Cardiff CF99 1NA (Information Line 029 2089 8200).

Trade union

If you were a member of a trade union before retirement, it may be worth contacting your local branch, particularly for problems over a pension from work.

Welfare rights and money advice centres

There may be an independent welfare rights or money advice centre locally. Money advice centres generally deal with debt problems and may accept referrals only from other agencies.

NATIONAL SOURCES OF HELP

The national organisations listed below may be able to help or put you in touch with a source of advice.

Association of Charity Officers (incorporating the Occupational Benevolent Funds Alliance)
Beechwood House
Wyllyotts Close
Potters Bar
Hertfordshire EN6 2HW
Tel: 01707 651777
Provides information about charities that make grants to individuals in need.

Carers UK
20–25 Glasshouse Yard
London EC1A 4JT
Tel: 020 7490 8818
Helpline: 0808 808 7777, weekdays 10.00am–12.00pm and 2.00pm–4.00pm
Website: www.carersnorth.demon.co.uk
Provides general advice and help for all carers.

Charity Search
25 Portview Road
Avonmouth
Bristol BS11 9LD
Tel: 0117 982 4060, weekdays 10.00am–4.00pm
Helps link older people with charities that may provide grants to individuals. Applications in writing are preferred.

Counsel and Care
Twyman House
16 Bonny Street
London NW1 9PG
Tel: 020 7485 1550

Advice line (local rate call): 0845 300 7585, weekdays
10.00am–12.30am and 2.00pm–4.00 pm
Website: www.counselandcare.org.uk

*Advises on obtaining and paying for residential and nursing
home care.*

Disability Alliance
Universal House
88–94 Wentworth Street
London E1 7SA
Tel: 020 7247 8776
Rights advice line: 020 7247 8763, Mondays and Wednesdays
2.00pm–4.00pm
Website: www.disabilityalliance.org

Produces Disability Rights Handbook *(see page 155) and other
publications and gives advice on social security benefits for
disabled people through the Rights Advice Line.*

Energy Action Grants Agency
Eldon Court
Eldon Square
Newcastle Upon Tyne NE1 7HA
Freephone: 0800 072 0150
Website: www.eaga.co.uk

*Administers the Home Energy Efficiency Scheme and 'The Warm
Deal' in Scotland (described on pages 114–115).*

foundations
Bleaklow House
Howard Town Mills
Glossop SK13 8HT
Tel: 01457 891909
Website: www.foundations.uk.com

*The national co-ordinating body for home improvement
agencies.*

Pensions Advisory Service (OPAS)
11 Belgrave Road
London SW1V 1RB
Helpline: 0845 601 2923
Website: www.opas.org.uk

Offers help and advice about occupational and personal pensions. Will deal directly with the scheme provider if the problem requires. Can also deal with general enquiries about State pensions.

Royal National Institute of the Blind (RNIB)
105 Judd Street
London WC1H 9NE
Tel: 020 7388 1266
Helpline: 0845 766 9999, weekdays 9.00am–5.00pm
Website: www.rnib.org.uk/lowvision

The Benefits Advice and Information Team offers advice and information on social security issues for blind and partially sighted people. The phone number in Wales is 029 2045 0440.

Royal National Institute for Deaf People (RNID)
RNID Information Line
19–23 Featherstone Street
London EC1Y 8SL
Tel: 020 7296 8000 (general)
Helpline: 0808 808 0123, 9.00 am–5.00 pm
Textphone: 0808 808 9000
Website: www.rnid.org.uk

Provides information for deaf people. The phone number in Wales is 029 2033 3034.

For information about national organisations in Scotland, Wales and Northern Ireland, contact the appropriate national Age Concern (addresses on page 157).

FURTHER READING

Government leaflets

As well as the leaflets mentioned in *Your Rights*, there is a catalogue of all the social security leaflets produced (Cat 1). Social security leaflets should be available from your local social security office, and they are sometimes in libraries, post offices or CABs. Many are also available on the Internet at www.dwp.gov.uk. The Inland Revenue deals with issues relating to NI contributions. Leaflets on contributions can be obtained from either social security or Inland Revenue offices or on the Internet at www.inlandrevenue.gov.uk. Leaflets on help with health costs are available from the Department of Health, PO Box 777, London SE1 6XH, on the Internet at www.doh.gov.uk or by ringing the Health Literature Line on 0800 555 777.

Other publications

For detailed information on services and benefits for disabled people, you may wish to get the *Disability Rights Handbook 2002–2003*, £13 (£9 for individuals receiving any State benefits), available from the Disability Alliance, Universal House, 88–94 Wentworth Street, London E1 7SA. Tel: 020 7247 8776.

For detailed information on all social security benefits, with reference to the relevant Government legislation, you may wish to refer to the *2002–2003 Welfare Benefits Handbook*, £25 plus £3 post and packing (£7 plus £1 post and packing for benefit claimants), which is available from the Child Poverty Action Group (CPAG), 94 White Lion Street, London N1 9PF. Tel: 020 7837 7979. This two volume book covers both means-tested and non-means-tested benefits.

These books may also be available for reference at your local library.

KEEPING UP TO DATE

Your Rights is based on the information available at the beginning of March 2002 and the benefit levels will normally apply until the first week in April 2003. A new edition of the book will be published next year to cover the period from April 2003 to April 2004. However, sometimes changes are made during the course of a year.

If you would like us to inform you of any major changes introduced before April 2003, please cut off this page and return it to the address below.

Write in with your details if you do not want to cut up the book.

Dear Age Concern

Please send me details about any major changes introduced before April 2003

Name (block letters) _____

Signature _____

Address _____

_____

_____

Postcode _____

Please return to:

Age Concern
FREEPOST (SWB 30375)
Ashburton
Devon TQ13 7ZZ

ABOUT AGE CONCERN

Your Rights: A guide to money benefits for older people is one of a wide range of publications produced by Age Concern England, the National Council on Ageing. Age Concern works on behalf of all older people and believes that later life should be fulfilling and enjoyable. For too many this is impossible. As the leading charitable movement in the UK concerned with ageing and older people, Age Concern finds effective ways to change that situation.

Where possible, we enable older people to solve problems themselves, providing as much or as little support as they need. A network of local Age Concerns, supported by 250,000 volunteers, provides community-based services such as lunch clubs, day centres and home visiting.

Nationally, we take a lead role in campaigning, parliamentary work, policy analysis, research, specialist information and advice provision, and publishing. Innovative programmes promote healthier lifestyles and provide older people with opportunities to give the experience of a lifetime back to their communities.

Age Concern is dependent on donations, covenants and legacies.

Age Concern England
1268 London Road
London SW16 4ER
Tel: 020 8765 7200
Fax: 020 8765 7211

Age Concern Cymru
4th Floor
1 Cathedral Road
Cardiff CF11 9SD
Tel: 029 2037 1566
Fax: 029 2039 9562

Age Concern Scotland
113 Rose Street
Edinburgh EH2 3DT
Tel: 0131 220 3345
Fax: 0131 220 2779

Age Concern Northern Ireland
3 Lower Crescent
Belfast BT7 1NR
Tel: 028 9024 5729
Advice line: 028 9032 5055
(10am–1pm)
Fax: 028 9023 5497

PUBLICATIONS FROM AGE CONCERN BOOKS

Money matters

Your Taxes and Savings 2002–2003
Paul Lewis

The definitive annual guide to financial planning for older people, this popular book:

- is fully revised and updated
- explains the tax system in clear, concise language
- describes the range of saving and investment options available
- includes model portfolios to illustrate a range of financial scenarios

Your Taxes and Savings explains how the tax system affects people over retirement age, including how to avoid paying more tax than necessary.

£5.99 0-86242-352-X

Using Your Home as Capital 2002–2003
Cecil Hinton and David McGrath

This best-selling book for homeowners, which is updated annually, gives a detailed explanation of how to capitalise on the value of your home and obtain a regular additional income.

£4.99 0-86242-353-8

The Pensions Handbook 2002–2003: Planning ahead to boost retirement income
Sue Ward

Many older people in their later working lives become concerned about the adequacy of their existing pension arrangements. This annually updated title addresses these worries and suggests strategies to enhance the value of a prospective pension.

£6.99 0-86242-354-6

General

Managing Debt: A guide for older people
Edited by Yvonne Gallacher and Jim Gray
A significant proportion of older people continue to experience financial problems in retirement. This comprehensive book aims to help those people break free from the vicious debt cycle. It provides information, advice and guidance on managing debt. Topics covered in detail include:

- getting into debt
- negotiating with creditors
- money advice
- prioritising debts and dealing with emergencies
- bankruptcy
- understanding the law and your rights

Written in clear, jargon free language, the book contains examples, sample letters, case studies and a glossary of terms, and is a complete self-help guide for people with financial problems.
£7.99 0-86242-236-1

Changing Direction: Employment options in mid-life: 2nd edition
Sue Ward
Redundancy or early retirement can come as a shock to anybody, but the impact in mid-life can be devastating. The new edition of this topical and highly practical book is designed to help those aged 40–55 get back to work. Always positive and upbeat, it examines issues such as adjusting to change, finances, opportunities for work, deciding what work you really want to do and working for yourself.
£9.99 0-86242-331-7

The Retirement Handbook: 3rd edition
Ro Lyon
A comprehensive handbook for older people on the point of retirement, this book is full of practical information and advice on all the opportunities available. It also points readers in the right direction to obtain more information when required. Drawing on Age Concern's wealth of experience, it covers everything you need to know, including:

- managing your money
- staying healthy
- using your time
- leisure activities
- housing options
- relationships

The *Retirement Handbook* is easy to use and designed to encourage everyone to view retirement as an opportunity not to be missed.
£7.99 0-86242-350-3

Healthy Eating on a Budget
Sara Lewis and Dr Juliet Gray
Opening with a comprehensive introduction to achieving a nutritionally balanced diet, this book contains 100 plus closely costed recipes for the health-conscious cook, all of which are flagged up to show their nutritional values and calorie content.
£6.95 0-86242-170-5

Health and care

The Carers Handbook Series
The Carers Handbook Series has been written for the families and friends of older people. It guides you through the key stages of a crisis and helps you take practical, informed decisions.

Caring for Someone with an Alcohol Problem
Mike Ward
More people drink alcohol than smoke, gamble or use illegal drugs. When drinking becomes a problem, the consequences for the carer can often be so physically and emotionally exhausting that it is difficult to see any way out of the situation. This book will be of invaluable help to anyone who lives with or cares for a problem drinker, with particular emphasis on the problems of caring for an older problem drinker.
£6.99 0-86242-227-2

Caring for Someone at a Distance
Julie Spencer-Cingöz
People are now living longer than at any previous time in history, and this means that, sooner or later, we are likely to

find ourselves looking after a loved one or a friend – often at a distance. This book will help you to identify the needs and priorities that have to be addressed, offering guidance on the key decisions to be made, minimising risks, what to look for when you visit, how to get the most out of your visits, dealing with your relative's finances and keeping in touch.
£6.99 0-86242-228-0

The Carer's Handbook: What to do and who to turn to
Marina Lewycka
At some point in their lives millions of people find themselves suddenly responsible for organising the care of an older person with a health crisis. All too often such carers have no idea what services are available or who can be approached for support. This book is designed to act as a first point of reference in just such an emergency, signposting readers on to many more detailed, local sources of advice.
£6.99 0-86242-262-0

Finding and Paying for Residential and Nursing Home Care
Marina Lewycka
Acknowledging that an older person needs residential care often represents a major crisis for family and friends. Feelings of guilt and betrayal invariably compound the difficulties faced in identifying a suitable care home and sorting out the financial arrangements. This book provides a practical step-by-step guide to the decisions which have to be made and the help which is available.
£6.99 0-86242-261-2

Choices for the Carer of an Elderly Relative
Marina Lewycka
Being a carer may mean many different things – from living at a distance and keeping a check on things by telephone to taking on a full-time caring role. This book looks at the choices facing someone whose parent or other relative needs care. It helps readers to look at their own circumstances and their own priorities and decide what is the best role for themselves – as well as the person being cared for.
£6.99 0-86242-263-9

Caring for Someone with Arthritis
Jim Pollard

This book is aimed at someone who is either caring or considering caring for a person with arthritis and raises many of the practical and personal issues involved. It examines what arthritis actually is, how it can be treated, the role of the carer and long-term planning.

£6.99 0-86242-266-3

Caring for Someone with a Heart Problem
Toni Battison

This book offers practical information, advice and support to people who care for someone with coronary heart disease. It explains how the heart works, and what the term coronary heart disease means. It considers the range of lifestyle changes that can be made to help to manage the condition, and suggests how some complementary therapies can be used to reduce stress levels. There is also valuable information on the help that is available to carers from statutory and voluntary organisations. Designed as a first point of reference, *Caring for Someone with a Heart Problem* contains clear, practical information and advice, checklists and useful addresses, and will serve as an invaluable guide for readers in need of advice.

£6.99 0-86242-252-3

If you would like to order any of these titles, please write to the address below, enclosing a cheque or money order for the appropriate amount (plus £1.95 p&p) made payable to Age Concern England. Credit card orders may be made on 0870 44 22 044 (for individuals); or 0870 44 22 120 (AC federation, other organisations and institutions); Fax: 01626 323318.

Age Concern Books
PO Box 232
Newton Abbot
Devon TQ12 4XQ

INDEX

BENEFIT RATES APRIL 2002–2003

Some of the main weekly benefit rates are listed below for quick reference:

Attendance Allowance
higher rate	£56.25
lower rate	£37.65

Disability Living Allowance

care component
highest rate	£56.25
middle rate	£37.65
lowest rate	£14.90

mobility component
higher rate	£39.30
lower rate	£14.90

Income Support/Housing Benefit/Council Tax Benefit standard applicable amounts for people aged 60 or over*

single person	£98.15
couple	£149.80

Invalid Care Allowance £42.45

Incapacity Benefit (long-term rate) £70.95

Severe Disablement Allowance (basic rate) £42.80

Retirement pension
basic rate	£75.50
wife on husband's contributions	£45.20
couple on husband's contributions	£120.70

*See pages 45–53 for details of other premiums and housing costs which may give rise to higher rates.